THE SOCIOLOGY
OF JOURNALISM

BRIAN McNAIR

Reader in Film and Media Studies,
University of Stirling

A member of the Hodder Headline Group
LONDON • NEW YORK • SYDNEY • AUCKLAND

First published in Great Britain in 1998 by
Arnold, a member of the Hodder Headline Group,
338 Euston Road, London NW1 3BH

http://www.arnoldpublishers.com

Co-published in the United States of America by
Oxford University Press Inc.,
198 Madison Avenue, New York, NY10016

The advice and information in this book are believed to be true and
accurate at the date of going to press, but neither the author nor the
publisher can accept any legal responsibility or liability for any errors
or omissions.

British Library Cataloguing in Publication Data
A catalogue entry for this book is available from the British Library

Library of Congress Cataloging-in-Publication Data
McNair, Brian, 1959–
    The sociology of journalism / Brian McNair.
        p.   cm.
    Includes bibliographical references and index.
    ISBN 0-340-70616-3 (hb. : alk. paper). — ISBN 0-340-70615-5
(pbk. : alk. paper)
    1. Journalism—Social aspects.   2. Journalism—Great Britain.
I. Title.
PN4749.M36   1998
302.23—dc21   98-7067
                                                                  CIP

ISBN 0 340 70616 3 (hb)
ISBN 0 340 70615 5 (pb)

1 2 3 4 5 6 7 8 9 10

Production Editor: Rada Radojicic
Production Controller: Rose James
Cover Design: Terry Griffiths

Composition by Phoenix Photosetting, Chatham, Kent
Printed and bound in Great Britain by
MPG Books, Bodmin, Cornwall

Contents

Preface   vii

PART I   INTRODUCTIONS AND BACKGROUND

1   Introduction   3
2   The sociology of journalism   19
3   The effects of journalism   34

PART II   THE FACTORS OF JOURNALISTIC PRODUCTION

4   The professional culture and organisational determinants
    of journalism   61
5   The political environment   82
6   The economic environment   101
7   The technological environment   125
8   The sociology of sources   143
9   From control to chaos: towards a new sociology
    of journalism   162

Notes   167
Bibliography   173
Index   179

Preface

Although my academic roots (and my university degrees) are in sociology, I have never been a sociology lecturer. Rather, I have earned my living since graduation in the hybrid field of 'media studies', alongside historians, linguists, economists, social psychologists and all those others from diverse backgrounds whose work requires them to study the institutions of mass communication.

Media studies has always felt like the best place for me to be, as a sociologist, because there are no phenomena of greater importance to the life of contemporary capitalist societies than those associated with the media. For that reason, too, media studies is to present-day social science what sociology was in the 1960s and 1970s: on the intellectual cutting edge; radical and challenging; essential to an understanding of how modern societies work. The jealous, often juvenile, sniping at media studies which comes from other branches of academia, as well as from some in the media, is an echo of the abuse once experienced by sociology itself and should be worn by all those who teach, study and research media as a badge of honour; better the hostility of intellectual luddites than the marginalisation which comes with irrelevance.

Amongst the multiplicity of genres and forms which make up 'the media' none is of greater sociological importance than journalism, and I welcome the opportunity to reassert my academic roots by presenting this sociology of journalism to what will be in the main a media and communication studies readership.

This book does not presume any specialist foreknowledge of the discipline of sociology amongst its potential readers. It is written principally for students of the media who need to know something of the social determinants and impacts of journalistic texts but who are not necessarily going to take degrees in sociology. I have avoided sociological jargon where possible, therefore, in favour of an approach which aims to combine conceptual clarity with readability. I hope and trust, of course, that sociology and other social science students with an element of media studies in their programmes will also find the book useful.

Brian McNair
Stirling
August 1998

PART

I

INTRODUCTIONS AND BACKGROUND

1

Introduction

This is a book about journalism and its relationship to the societies within which it is produced: what my title describes as the *sociology* of journalism.

A sociology of journalism has two broad concerns. The first concern, and the subject matter of Part I of this book, is to understand the impact of journalistic media on, and their contribution to, the workings of contemporary capitalist societies, in particular those of the liberal democratic type such as the United States and Britain, from each of which this book draws for illustration of its main arguments. I have also included discussion of the 'new democracies' of central and eastern Europe, where liberal democratic notions of the journalist's role are being tested to the limit in the transition from economically centralised, politically authoritarian systems to capitalist economic and political organisation. Where appropriate, and for the purposes of comparison, the role of journalism in authoritarian societies of left and right, such as China and Saudi Arabia, is also considered.

A sociology of journalism is, second, interested in the *social* determinants of journalistic output – those features of social life and organisation which shape, influence and constrain its form and content. The sociologist of journalism assumes that his or her object of study both acts on, and is acted on by, the surrounding social environment. The journalistic text is viewed as the product of a wide variety of cultural, technological, political and economic forces, specific to a particular society at a particular time. Understanding the content, meaning, role and impact of journalism therefore requires description and analysis of the broader social context within which it is produced and of the *factors* of production which determine that context. These factors are examined in Part II of this book.

Journalism: a definition

Before we can begin to pursue these broad aims, however, a simple question requires an answer. What *is* journalism and, of equal relevance in this ambivalent postmodern world, what is not? When the dividing lines in contemporary culture between education, information and entertainment, between art and trash, between high and low, elite and mass, are not always clear, and usually contested, where is the line to be drawn between journalism and not-journalism, and does it matter?

It *does* matter, because the sociological significance of journalistic communication arises largely from the audience's expectations of a distinctive form and content and from their agreement that when these distinguishing characteristics are present the resulting communication enjoys a special status over others which are not journalistic. Journalism is in this sense a *privileged* cultural form and has been ever since the social upheavals of early modern Europe in which it first found a central place in public discourse. Its privileges are the reward for adherence to quite specific stylistic and narrative conventions, which I describe below.

Defining journalism is made more difficult by the tendency of many twentieth-century journalists deliberately to subvert the conventions of their chosen form, setting out to introduce into it qualities more commonly associated with art. The novelistic 'new journalism' of post-war America, exemplified by the work of Tom Wolfe, Hunter Thompson and others, or the cinematic scale of a documentary such as *When We Were Kings* (Leon Gast, 1996)[1] indicates the difficulty of setting up too-rigid categories which preclude the possibility of a journalist also being an artist, a scientist or even a sociologist. I will try here, nonetheless, to establish what it is that makes the work of the journalist distinct from those others.

Rather than work through the variety of definitions to be found elsewhere in the academic and professional literature, I will move quickly to defining journalism for the purposes of this book as:

> any *authored* text, in written, audio or visual form, which *claims* to be (i.e. is presented to its audience as) a *truthful* statement about, or record of, some *hitherto unknown* (new) feature of the *actual, social* world.

This definition, and the elements I have emphasised, allow us to distinguish journalism from other forms of cultural discourse which may be similar in some respects.

Truth

First, journalism lays claim to the qualities of truthfulness and accuracy – properties often implied by the term *objectivity*, a concept used to legitimise the journalistic text while at the same time recognising the multidimensional and elusive nature of 'truth' (see Chapter 4). Journalism asks to be accepted as, at the very least, an *approximation* to truth, and certainly close enough to the truth to be worthy of our trust in its integrity.

Newness

The journalistic statement also has to be new, if not in the facts presented then in the interpretation of (or 'spin' put on) those facts. Journalism tells us things we did not already know, as, of course, do listings of share prices on Wall Street, or yesterday's average temperatures in the world's capitals, but these and similar types of data, presented as columns of numbers on a page or a television screen, are not 'journalism' by my definition, because they are not authored. Many of the new on-line information services started by Microsoft and other companies which are alleged to threaten the future of print media (see Chapter 7) fall into this category and are often distinguished by their makers from 'real' journalism. Computers and their operators generate and assemble lists, without analysis, commentary or interpretation. They are immensely valuable to many groups of users, including journalists. Such data are perhaps the key strategic resource of capitalism in its current, information-dependent phase.[2] They become journalism, however, only when they are given meaning and context – when they are transformed into a story or narrative – by an author.

Authorship and ideology

No story can be told, no account of events given, without contextualisation around a set of assumptions, beliefs and values. This is in the nature of storytelling. To present a list of thermometer and barometer readings tells us something about the weather on a given day, but does not tell us a story (and is not journalism). To present the figures in the context of a narrative about 'good' and 'bad' weather does tell

us a story, however, and immediately introduces certain ideas and
value judgments about what 'good' and 'bad' means in weather
terms; ideas with which we may agree or disagree. These ideas com-
prise the framework within which events taking place in the world
beyond our immediate sensory experience can be made sense of, given
meaning and context temporally, geographically, and socially. In an
authored weather report (which should be considered as part of the
journalistic repertoire) scientific measurements of physical states are
given a historical meaning – 'the driest April this century', 'the biggest
storm since records began', etc. – and a significance in the wider social
world which is the rationale for the journalistic importance of the
information being reported.

Journalism, therefore, like any other narrative which is the work
of human agency, is essentially *ideological* – a communicative vehicle
for the transmission to an audience (intentionally or otherwise) not
just of facts but of the assumptions, attitudes, beliefs and values of its
maker(s), drawn from and expressive of a particular world-view. The
content of that ideology may be consciously and purposefully articulated, as when a newspaper proprietor uses his economic power to
determine editorial viewpoint, or 'bias' (see Chapter 6), or it may be
(as in the case of a public service broadcasting organisation such as
the British Broadcasting Corporation) a loosely structured distilla-
tion of the values deemed socially consensual by its producers at any
given time – an attempt to represent public or universal values as
opposed to private ideologies and interests.

In this sense journalism may also be viewed as an index of the balance of social forces in a society. Journalists construct their narratives
around their own values and beliefs, but these are necessarily
informed by the contributions of a wide range of information sources,
who thus acquire the power to become 'definers' of journalistic reality. Believable, 'true' journalism requires authentication and verifica-
tion by non-journalistic witnesses such as politicians, academics,
professional specialists and other accredited sources of information
and interpretation who lend their expert status to the text and give it
authority in the eyes of the audience. Moreover, the journalistic
demand for sources (as we shall henceforth refer to those whom journalists employ in this way), encourages contemporary social actors to
compete with ever-increasing sophistication and intensity for access
to the media, using techniques of what has come to be known as *public relations* or news management (see Chapter 8). Source activity can
thus be viewed as a means of ideological struggle.

The strength and power of sources can be inferred from their ability to 'make' the news, and to have their positions represented accurately. It may also be inferred by the extent to which the views of non-journalistic (extramedia) actors become part of the journalistic mainstream. For example, the emergence of environmental 'beats' within many journalistic organisations in the late 1980s, and the now routine identification of environmental damage as 'news' can be read as evidence that the environmentalist world-view, or ideology, has grown in strength and influence over time.[3] The incorporation of many such 'isms' into the ideological fabric of contemporary journalistic production is similarly expressive of changes in the socio-political environment which journalism reflects (for example, the now routine journalistic acceptance of sexism and racism as 'bad things').

So journalism, as an authored narrative, is at the same time an ideological force, communicating not just 'the facts' but also a way of understanding and making sense of the facts. And since there is likely to be more than one way of understanding and interpreting even the most apparently neutral of facts, journalism is thus an arena for struggle between competing ways of sense-making; an expression and reflection of the ideological 'balance of forces' in a given society, a balance which changes over time, owing at least partly to the exposure which journalism may give to ideas alternative to, even oppositional to, currently dominant ideas.

Actuality

Novelists and feature film directors are authors too, of course, who may claim to be making statements containing new or original truths, but in the context of *fictional, imaginary* worlds located in the past, present or future. These fictions may be intended to have lessons for the real worlds of their audiences but are distinct from journalistic texts in that they are not narratives of actuality, nor do they claim to be. Documentary film, on the other hand, or the book-length works of Hunter Thompson and Ryszard Kapuscinski,[4] may utilise aesthetic techniques familiar to fiction-writers but are generally viewed as journalism rather than fiction insofar as the stories they tell are (or are claimed to be) true stories about the world of existing people and events.[5]

Journalism and the social

Scientific discourse is another kind of authored narrative which, like journalism, aspires to embody truth about the actual world and will often do so in startlingly new and original terms. We would not claim Stephen Hawking's *A Brief History of Time* (1988) to be journalism, however. Science becomes the subject of journalism only when it impinges on the world of human beings. A hurricane is news not because it exists but because it threatens the social organisation of human beings somewhere on the planet. The natural world is news-worthy only in its *interaction* with the social. The comet Hale–Bopp became the subject of extensive journalistic interest in 1997 because, first, it was visible by human observers all over the world, second, it fitted into ongoing late-twentieth-century scientific and journalistic narrative frameworks about the possibility of extraterrestrial bodies such as comets and asteroids colliding with the earth, and, third, related to this, it prompted a considerable amount of end-of-mille-nium anxiety, exemplified when a group of religious cultists in California committed mass suicide.

Journalism is primarily about the *social* rather than the natural worlds, then. Scientific discourse, although often providing the raw material of journalistic narratives *about* science, is not in itself jour-nalism, dealing as it does with the actually existing *natural* rather than social world. Only when the natural world intervenes in or interferes with the social worlds of human beings does it become the subject of news as opposed to the preserve of science.

Social scientific discourses, on the other hand (history, economics, sociology), may be argued to have more in common with journalism as I am defining it here. Sociological writing, for example, seeks to reveal new knowledge about the social world we actually inhabit, and asks that its discoveries be trusted. Its methods are often similar to those of journalism (research, investigation, observation, interview-ing of sources) and, indeed, the barrier between journalism and social science is more easily crossed than that between journalism and nat-ural science. Much journalism (particularly 'features' journalism) is similar to social history, sociology or social psychology in content if not in form. The concerns of social science are often, and for obvious reasons, those of the journalist, but the two are distinct. The profes-sional social scientist, like the scientist of the natural world, is bound by academic codes of style and presentation from which the journal-ist is relatively free and which, in an era of ever-increasing specialisation, the mass of the audience is probably prevented from fully understanding. These lead to a discursive exclusivity and elitism which proclaim a particular and jealously protected status for social scientific narratives.

Although the best journalists may be excellent historians and sociologists, and the best social scientists may be comfortable writing for and appearing in journalistic media as *accredited witnesses*, the distinction remains one which professionals in both categories would intuitively recognise and which is widely acknowledged by media producers when using social scientists as sources in the construction of news and other forms of journalism.

A typology of journalism

Journalism, then, is not simply the presentation of new or useful data. What journalism is, or aspires to be, is revealed truth, *mediated reality*, an account of the existing, real world as appropriated by the journalist and processed in accordance with the particular requirements of the journalistic medium through which it will be disseminated to some section of the public. It lacks the empirical depth and methodological rigour of science, as it generally avoids the impressionism of art, although it may at times seek to impersonate either or both.

This attempt to limit what journalism is and is not allows us to include within the scope of the sociology which follows journalism in all its concrete manifestations: writing (in newspapers and periodicals and on the Internet); speech and sound (on radio and television); and the visual forms of photography, film and video, which can be edited to tell stories by themselves or combined with writing and speech to form accounts and depictions of events which have actually happened and of the social, economic and political implications of those events. It includes the following basic types of journalistic output:

- the *news report*, which aims simply to inform us about what is happening of importance and, of course, is in some sense *new* in the world around us;
- the *feature article*, which presents more in-depth reportage and analysis of a particular subject, and its broadcasting equivalent, the documentary[6] and current affairs programme;

- the *commentary* or *column*, in which a journalist presents his or her readers with an (assumed to be) authoritative viewpoint on a particular issue, and its equivalent in broadcasting, the output of the specialist pundit;
- the *interview*, probing the views and policies of those *in* the news, especially politicians and celebrities;
- the *editorial*, in which a newspaper or periodical 'speaks out' in its 'public voice'. (Television and radio journalists rarely editorialise, for reasons to be explored later.)

Each of these discursive types, with their distinctive rhetorical styles, aesthetic conventions and communicative functions, contributes to the totality of what journalism is – at one and the same time a large, profitable, and ever-expanding sector of the media market, the key source of information about the environment in which we live (physical and social) and an essential element in the maintenance and management of political, economic and social relations.

That journalism is all of these things, as well as a resource for recreation and entertainment, became true when mass media were firmly established as central economic, political and cultural institutions at the beginning of the twentieth century. The spread of the Internet and digital communication technologies in the twenty-first century will see information confirmed as the most important global resource, and journalism as the dominant mode of cultural expression in advanced capitalist societies.

About this book

Its obvious centrality in contemporary culture naturally makes the journalistic profession seem an attractive destination for the growing numbers of young people who study the media, first at school, then in colleges and universities throughout the world. Journalism is not quite 'the new rock 'n' roll' (although Hunter Thompson and some of the 'new journalists' enjoyed rock star status in the 1960s and 1970s), but each country has its own journalistic superstars who enjoy the status of senior politicians (without the responsibilities of office), the glamour of celebrities (without, except in rare cases, the irritating attentions of the paparazzi) and the salaries of top businessmen (without the need to show a profit at the end of their working day). Although the majority of journalists work for modest salaries, in conditions of low job security and unsettlingly rapid technological change, the profession nevertheless enjoys high prestige and glamour; this despite the fact of opinion polls which regularly show that, like politicians and lawyers, journalists as a group are somewhat disliked and distrusted by the public, and for reasons that are not difficult to understand. The corrupt tabloid parasites depicted in Gordon Burn's novel *Fullalove* (1996) and Billy Wilder's classic 1951 movie *The Big Carnival* (released as *Ace In The Hole* in Britain), or the paparazzi who chased Princess Diana to her death in August 1997, exist in the public imagination alongside the noble defenders of truth who exposed the Watergate cover-up. The *Guardian*'s exposure between 1994 and 1996 of British members of parliament who took bribes[7] was countered by the *Sun*'s ill-judged publication in 1996 of crudely faked video footage of the late Princess Diana in 'love romps'. Modern journalism has its negative as well as positive attributes, and there are many in the audience, as well as academics, politicians and professional journalists themselves, who believe that the former now predominate in the overall product mix, with negative social consequences.[8]

Whether the reality of their intended profession justifies it or not, the prospect of being disliked and distrusted is apparently no disincentive to those thousands of media students who see a successful career in journalism as their goal. Nor should it be, since unpopularity is often the fate of the bringer of bad tidings (and good news, as Chapter 4 shows, is usually no news). But no matter how unpopular journalists may be as a professional group, the fact remains that journalism as a commodity is irrepressibly, unquenchably in demand. The number of journalistic outlets – print and electronic – continues to expand, and the market for journalism of all kinds shows no signs of shrinking. The arrival on the mass market of digital television, and the establishment of the Internet as a mass medium, has given another powerful boost to a communicative form which began with the invention of the printing press in the fifteenth century and has harnessed each new technological innovation to its aims ever since.

The dawning of a new technological era, which happens to coincide with the beginning of a new millenium, is a particularly appropriate point at which to examine the processes by which journalism is made; to understand why it takes the forms it does, and why some events and not others become the subject of journalistic discourse. This book seeks to do all of these things, as well as to provide those with an interest in journalism – be it professional, academic or lay – with a knowledge of the factors and forces which contribute to its construction. For sociology asserts that there is something innately *social* about all the phenomena which are its objects of study – that there are social factors and processes underpinning the evolution of common sense categories such as 'mental illness', 'crime' or indeed 'journalism'. For some sociologists, for example, the condition known as 'schizophrenia', despite widespread use of the term by the psychiatric profession, is not best approached as an illness in the recognised sense of that term (it has no universally agreed aetiology, symptoms or treatment) but as a socially constructed label applied to people who do not behave 'normally' and who display certain behavioural and psychological characteristics which have come to be understood as 'schizophrenic' (and which do of course cause them real problems in the social world). The difference is not a pedantic one. As R.D. Laing powerfully argued in the 1960s, one person's mental illness may be another person's perfectly intelligible response to intolerable social circumstances, and understanding this may often be the key to a 'cure'.[9]

The point to note here is the extent to which the form and content of the categories through which we come to know the world are not natural, nor inevitable, but *socially determined*. In relation to our present discussion we might say that there is no universal, *objective* journalism (and we will discuss the social function of the concept of objectivity in detail in Chapter 4), only journal*isms*, with different styles and hierarchies of news values, shaped by and specific to particular societies at particular times. The sociologist declares that journalism in all its forms is, despite its claims to truthfulness, above all a *construction*: an intellectual product embodying the technological, economic, political and cultural histories of the societies within which it is produced, inexplicable without knowledge of those histories, and impossible to interpret correctly without the context which they provide. The sociology of journalism presented in this book describes that context and analyses the social relationships and interactions which define journalists' parameters of vision, constrain their autonomy, and shape – sometimes dictate – the form and content of what they write and speak about the world. Journalists in modern capitalist societies aspire to independence, and most have it to varying degrees, but they can never be entirely 'free' from the circumstances within which their work is organised, regulated, marketed and consumed. This book describes those circumstances and seeks to assess their relative influence on the output of the journalistic media.

Outline

The book proceeds in two stages. Following this introduction, Chapter 2 considers the normative roles and functions of journalism in liberal democratic societies, and the sociological critique of those normative ideas. The chapter ends by positioning this book in relation to that debate.

We then move on in Chapter 3 to an examination of journalism's impacts, influences and effects on society, broadly defined. What are the social consequences, intended or otherwise, of journalistic activity, on individuals, groups and institutions? Are they desirable or undesirable and what, depending on the answer to that question, can be done to mitigate or enhance them?

The second part of the book describes the social determinants of journalistic media in contemporary capitalist societies such as the United States and Britain, authoritarian societies of the ideological left and right and the emerging democracies of the post-Soviet and developing (or 'third') world – what Klaus Bruhn-Jensen calls 'the social factors [which] make themselves known in news organisations in the form of economic, bureaucratic, and normative pressures which shape journalistic work'(1986, p. 49). I have divided these factors into five categories, as shown in Figure 1.1.

- The first factor of production to be discussed is the system of professional ethics, aesthetic codes and routine practices which guide journalistic work. Some of these, such as the ethic of objectivity, have their origins in the scientific and philosophical revolutions of the nineteenth century, whereas others – the prevailing system of newsvalues, for example – have evolved over time, changing in response to market conditions, technological innovation and consequent changes in the bureacratic and managerial demands of the modern newsroom.

- Second (and the order of their presentation here does not imply any assessment of their relative importance in shaping content, since this will vary across time and between societies), journalists are influenced by politicians, and the political systems within which they work. These shape the censorship, regulatory and governmental information management regimes in a given society and also define the more fluid environmental feature of 'political culture'. In post-Soviet Russia, as we shall see, press freedom exists in theory, but journalists are so rooted in the lingering political cul-

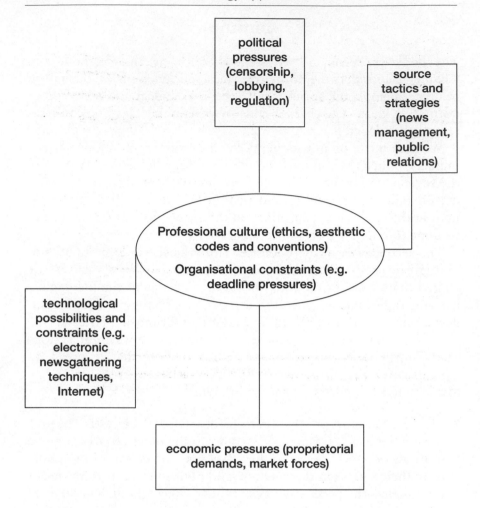

Figure 1.1 The social determinants of journalism

tures of authoritarianism and partisanship that they often find it difficult to practise 'freedom' as that term is understood in mature capitalist societies such as Britain or the United States.

- A third production factor is the influence of economics on journalism, and particularly the mechanism of economic ownership and control. Economic domination of media organisations is widely assumed to translate easily and clearly into cultural power, through the exercise of proprietorial influence over such key organisational features as personnel recruitment and editorial bias. Chapter 6 will analyse the extent of proprietorial power in the contemporary media environment, assess its limitations and examine how it is exercised on working journalists.

A further economic factor is the influence of evolving media and information markets on the content of journalism. In capitalist societies journalism is a *commodity* which must be sold to sophisticated and demanding consumers in an increasingly competitive marketplace. This economic fact of life has a major impact on the form, content and style of journalism, as we shall see. The market for popular tabloids is very different from the elite broadsheet sector, for example, a difference seen in structures of news values, writing styles and approaches to design. Marketing is now acknowledged to be central to the success of journalism, from the use of focus groups to the design of studio sets and presenters' clothing.

- The work of journalists is strongly influenced, fourth, by the technologies of newsgathering and production which they have at their disposal. The introduction of new information and communication technologies significantly affects the gathering, production and distribution of news and journalism in ways which we examine in Chapter 7.
- Fifth and finally, journalistic discourse is shaped by the information management activities of *extramedia* social actors (i.e. individuals or their organisations which are not themselves part of the media). This group includes politicians, pressure group activists, celebrities of sport and screen, public organisations such as the police and trade unions, and all other categories of social actor who seek to have their views journalistically represented in the most positive manner possible (from their self-interested perspectives). The increasing importance of this factor in recent years has given rise to a 'sociology of sources' within the broader sociology of journalism,[10] reflecting the recognition of analysts that the processes and practices of information management are central to the understanding of contemporary journalism. Chapter 8 of this book examines why 'source strategies' and news management tactics have become so important – what they involve and how effective they are in achieving the goals of those who employ them.

This categorisation of the production factors influencing journalism is clearly imperfect. Some factors – the lobbying activities of political spin doctors, for example – may fall into more than one of the categories shown in Figure 1.1 (such lobbying is both a specifically political pressure and a form of source activity comparable to that engaged in by corporations or trade unions). Likewise, it is not always clear if the editorial biases of the press are driven by economic pressures (to protect markets, for example) or by proprietorial commitment to a particular ideology. Sometimes, as we shall see, it is both. Although political and economic factors are analytically distinguishable, they often merge and interact. Economic relationships often have political significance, and vice versa. The spheres of politics and economics are connected.

Traditionally, the media studies literature has tended to overcome this difficulty by grouping the study of the influences exerted by politics and economics into one, the *politico-economic* approach.[11] My separation of them here does not imply a criticism of the politico-economic model of journalistic production as advanced by Peter Golding, Graham Murdock, James Curran and others. Rather, it reflects my feeling that the term has become too restrictive for an era when both the economic and the political pressures on journalists – including those, such as the British public service broadcasters, who were once relatively sheltered from them – are more intense and potentially overpowering than ever before.

My separation of the political and the economic for the purposes of the following discussion also acknowledges the fact that, in the post-cold-war era – the era of ideological 'triangulation' in the United States and the 'radical centre' in Britain – the chain of connection and causality between the interests of actors in the political and economic spheres on the one hand and their cultural expression in the content of journalism on the other is less obvious than was once the case.

Given that some overlap between these five sets of factors will be inevitable, then, it is nevertheless useful to break down the total social environment within which journalism is produced into distinct and empirically observeable spheres of agency. In doing so we may begin to assess the relative importance of politics, economics, technology and so on in shaping the overall 'product mix' and to understand and empathise with the reasons why journalism takes a particular form and content. Understanding does not preclude criticism, of course, but, by taking account of the practitioners' position and viewpoint, it does enable criticism to be more meaningful and constructive.

Using this book

I begin from an assumption that I hope will be shared by all readers of this book – that journalism is a key resource in supporting our role as citizens in societies which claim to value the democratic process. If that is true we clearly have an interest in understanding how it works, in being able to read it intelligently and to criticise it when necessary. This book aims to provide readers with the tools to do those things a little better in the belief that the best defence against any power which the oft-criticised journalistic media may have over our lives is informed scepticism. As Chapter 3 shows, there are many approaches to understanding the effects of journalism on society. None has produced empirical 'proof' of the kind that would satisfy a natural scientist, not least because sociological phenomena are rarely amenable to neat or numerical 'solutions', but I and many others would not study and write about journalism if we did not believe it to be an important and powerful cultural force. Checking and balancing that power is crucial to the maintenance of democratic capitalism, and implies at the very least a media-literate, critically competent audience able to contextualise and, on occasion, exercise the choice of *disbelief* in the truth of what it reads, sees and hears in the journalistic media. This book will have achieved its aims if it can contribute to and support the establishment and maintenance of such an audience.

For those vocationally motivated readers, on the other hand, who may wish eventually to pursue a career in journalism or a related occupation (public relations, for example) I hope that it will give an insight into the roots of, and rationales behind, many of the processes involved in modern journalism. John Hartley has complained that 'rarely do journalism courses ask their students to consider the conditions for journalism's existence: where it comes from, what it is for, and how it works' (1996, p. 35). This book and the Sociology of Journalism course at Stirling University on which it is based ask precisely those questions and aim to provide some answers too.

As well as forming a learning resource, however, the following pages contain an argument constructed around and in response to prevailing lines of critical thinking about journalism and its role in society. Those approaches, and the substance of this book's position in relation to them, are the subject of the next chapter. Here, I will say that if there is a theme running through the following pages it is that the elements which shape contemporary journalistic communication are tending to produce social instability and political unpredictability rather than, as has traditionally been argued by sociologists of journalism, conservative ideological control and systemic stability in favour of some 'ruling class' or establishment, and that the relationship of journalism to the powerful in advanced capitalist societies is increasingly subversive rather than supportive. The Monica Lewinsky scandal, which engulfed the Clinton presidency just as I was completing this book, lends support to the view expressed within it that the quantity of journalistic information now in mass circulation, and the speed of its flow, has created a media system which in effect, if not in intention, is profoundly unsympathetic or at least indifferent to the interests of those in society's elite positions.

Not everyone welcomes this trend, and there are many who connect it with the 'dumbing down' of journalism alleged to be a central feature of late twentieth-century news culture.[12] For others, including this writer, the growing unpredictability and irreverence of news media provides grounds for relative optimism about the democratic, watchdog role of the journalist in the new millenium.

|2|

The sociology of journalism

Traditionally, the sociology of journalism has taken the form of a debate between two ways of looking at how the social world is organised and the role of the media in sustaining that organisation. We can refer to them respectively as the paradigms of *competition* and *dominance*. The competitive paradigm has been associated with what we will also refer to as the *normative* approach – that is, that which expresses the *ideal*, or how things are *supposed to be*. The dominance paradigm, on the other hand, has been the province of *critical* analysts, who would argue that they focus on *things as they are*, and the gaps between the real and the ideal.

The competitive paradigm

Those whose perspectives on the role of journalism are structured by the competitive (or normative) paradigm view advanced, liberal capitalist societies of the North American and Western European type as arenas of essentially equal competition between diverse groups of social actors, for whom the media function as resource and representative both – supplying information, articulating opinions and helping to resolve political and ideological differences through the facilitation and organisation of public debate. The editorial and stylistic diversity of the press, for example, is viewed from this perspective as an expression and embodiment of the intellectual freedom which characterises liberal capitalism, articulating and making possible the pluralism of its politics and culture.

In this model the journalistic media are also watchdogs, comprising in their collective function a 'fourth estate': an independent institutional source of political and cultural power which monitors and scrutinises the actions of the powerful in other spheres. The concept of the fourth estate – the term was coined by the English political philosopher and pioneering theorist of liberal democracy, Edmund Burke, in the late eighteenth century[1] – recognised that there were established social classes in society – *estates* – whose potentially selfish use and abuse of their powers required limiting by society as a whole, or by those independent voices who could take on the task of representing society as a whole in the political process.

Journalistic independence to carry out these functions has been guaranteed, from this perspective, by two principal mechanisms. In the case of the privately-owned press and electronic media, economic ownership brings financial independence from the state, while diversity of media ownership within a particular capitalist economy guarantees plurality of journalistic viewpoint and the genuine competition of ideas.

Those media which are not privately owned (a declining proportion of the media sector as a whole) will usually have their political independence guaranteed by the constitution (written or unwritten) and organise their output within various notions of service to the public. The world's best known public service journalistic organisation, on which many others are modelled, is, of course, the British Broadcasting Corporation (BBC), whose proclamations of 'neutrality and impartiality' constitute a different kind of mechanism (from private ownership) for guaranteeing independence. The BBC is funded by the British taxpayer and is independent of the government of the day, at least in theory (as Chapter 5 shows, political pressure can influence a nominally independent organisation such as the BBC, but this is a deviation from the ideal, to the extent that it has in the past become a news story in itself). By serving no political or commercial master, the argument goes, the BBC has since its establishment in the 1920s serviced pluralistic democracy in the United Kingdom by reporting events and issues from a uniquely non-partisan position, only abandoning its neutrality (in temporary deference to the government of the day) when the nation-state itself has been perceived to be under threat, such as during the years of the Second World War.

In the United States, and other countries where broadcast journalism is commercialised, the main providers (ABC, NBC, CBS, Fox, CNN) present their output as being independent of political parties and of government and free from proprietors' or advertisers' interference in editorial matters. The pursuit of the 'public interest' in broadcast journalism is recognised in the United States, as it is in the case of the public service broadcasters of Western Europe, to be a key element in the maintenance of pluralistic liberal democracy, even if the legal, regulatory and institutional routes to achieving this goal will vary from country to country.

The contemporary significance of journalism's place in the preservation of pluralism derives from the role played by the emerging print media in the transition from feudalism to capitalism in early modern Europe.[2] In this lengthy historical process, which began in the late sixteenth century and culminated with the French Revolution of 1789, the first newspapers were the principal means by which the radical bourgeois developed, articulated and disseminated its liberal political and economic doctrines against the opposition of feudal despotisms and religious mythology. In the course of that struggle the defence of pluralism, political independence and intellectual freedom came to be associated with the routine practice of journalism in capitalism and has been accepted as a benchmark of high journalistic standards ever since.

The theory of liberal pluralism which underpins the competitive paradigm, as I have described it here, remains to this day the preferred model of how journalism works in advanced capitalist societies – preferred, that is, by those for whom the kind of capitalist society we live in today is, if not the best of all possible worlds, very nearly the best we can reasonably expect. Within it, to repeat, the journalist is depicted as a servant of the public interest. Even those working in the commercial media sector are viewed as necessary, socially useful elements of a system which taken as a whole provides for genuine competition of thought, opinion and ideology and thus makes the United States and other comparable countries combine to provide citizens with freedom of choice in their sources of news and analyses, from which they can go on to participate in the democratic process. The journalistic media supply information, forming collectively what many analysts now call 'public spheres', after the German theorist Jürgen Habermas[3] – communally accessible communicative spaces in which information, ideas and opinions can be debated and exchanged as a precondition for rational collective decision-making.

The dominance paradigm

Unfortunately, the theory of liberal pluralism which lies at the heart of the competitive paradigm, with its ideal of equal intellectual competition, has not always been matched by the practical performance of the media in capitalist systems, which even in their most advanced forms appear to all but the most blinkered observer as societies characterised by exploitation, injustice and thus inequality. In capitalism the abstract liberal notion of 'equal competition' is fundamentally constrained by the concrete realities of capital accumulation and the accompanying forms of social stratification, which lead to major inequalities in the distribution of economic resources, education and political power amongst the population of any and every capitalist society, no matter how advanced and civilised it has become. These inequalities of life-chance, in turn, generate social tensions and pressures which must be managed, in the context of relations of domination and subordination between the various categories which structure the social stratification system. The liberal pluralist ideal has little to say about the role of the media in managing these tensions and social relationships beyond asserting that since all citizens have a more or less equal right to have their views expressed and debated social problems can be negotiated to the satisfaction of all.

Opposed to the competitive model, then, are a variety of approaches to the social role of journalism which can be grouped together within the _dominance_ paradigm. This approach asserts that, rather than facilitating equal competition between diverse ideas and value systems, journalism is part of a cultural apparatus, the primary function of which is to maintain relations of domination and subordination between fundamentally _unequal_ groups in society who would, in the absence of such an apparatus, tear each other, their exploiters and the social fabric as a whole to pieces. Journalism in this model serves not the public, either as individuals or formed into groups confronting each other in equal competition, but the _dominant, private, selfish_ interests of a society stratified along lines of class, sex and ethnicity, to list three criteria of differential resource allocation familiar to all who live in capitalist systems.

All human societies are bound together by sets of agreed values and core beliefs – _ideologies_ – which function to regulate relationships and behaviour in the various spheres which constitute a human life – social, professional, financial, sexual. Ideologies can be thought of as the 'cement' which does this binding; the content and substance of the value systems which underpin a society, helping it manage its tensions and conflicts in a manner consistent with successful social reproduction. Judaeo-Christian religion, for example, has regulated sexual behaviour throughout four centuries of capitalist social organisation, favouring a particular form of family life which has been, whatever its constraints and limitations, broadly functional for capitalist development.[4] The ideology of 'freedom', expressed in relation to commerce, intellectual activity or political and cultural life, has for more than three hundred years legitimised a particular form of economic and political activity which is peculiar to capitalism, expressing the conditions of existence of its dominant groups.

The origination and intellectual elaboration of ideology is the subject of a whole branch of sociology. For our purposes we can think of it first as the work of philosophers, economists, religious leaders and other authorised thinkers, who have their ideas taken up and popularised by social organisations such as political parties and lobby groups. These latter use the cultural institutions of the media to articulate their views and promote their platforms, in competition with others. The media thus disseminate ideology on behalf of the groups whom they report and publicise, and indeed this is acknowledged to be one of the core functions of journalism in liberal democracy. But the media also function as an outlet for communicating the *already existing* ideological or value system: the cultural consensus prevailing in a given society at a given time. Media workers, like everyone else in society, adhere with more or less willingness and certainty to a set of values which are embodied in their output, structuring or 'framing' their accounts of the world.

Journalism has this effect (Chapter 3), plays this role, whether its practitioners are aware of it or not, just as in different ways and in different arenas parents communicate values to their children, ministers of the church to their flocks and college professors to their students. Journalists, indeed, have been collectively described as 'the new priesthood' in recognition of this aspect of their social role.

Whereas the competitive model stresses the underpinning equality and public-interest-driven nature of this ideological work, from the perspective of the dominance paradigm it is done in the context of a society divided into dominant and subordinate groups. As John Fiske puts it, journalists produce a 'dominant discourse' which 'serves dominant social interests' (1996, p. 5). The 'effect' of journalism is to reproduce this legitimising and rationalising discourse across social boundaries and over time. To use the language of critical social theory, the journalistic media are defined as part of the ideological apparatus of the capitalist state, reinforcing the values of the dominant groups within that state and ensuring their reproduction. To the extent that the media are perceived as purveyors of truth, journalistic discourse enjoys a persuasive power which can influence the structure of ideas circulating in a given society.

The media, although by no means the only set of institutions which facilitate the top-down transmission and social reproduction of dominant ideas in this model, are certainly one of the most important. Journalism in particular, with its special status as truthful information about the real world (see Chapter 1), fits into the model to the extent that its accounts of the world are assumed to be shaped and informed by the perspectives of the dominant groups in society.

There are three broad categories of mechanism by which this dominance is achieved. The first is *economic* (see Chapter 6). Material wealth, concentrated in the hands of a few individuals and organisations, buys ownership of media institutions, allowing direct proprietorial intervention in editorial policy, down to the level of 'spiking' – or more likely, not commissioning – unwanted or inconvenient stories. For those economically privileged individuals and organisations who do not themselves own media, economic power gives privileged access to the means of influencing media, such as the command of advertising resources or the employment of public relations specialists (see Chapter 8).

A second category of control mechanism is *political* – the law-making, censoring, regulatory and otherwise intimidatory powers of governments, which even in the most liberal democratic of countries are regularly deployed against the unruly media on behalf of big business, the government or the state itself (see Chapter 5). Sometimes, as during the Thatcher era in Britain, a tight alliance develops between government and key sectors of the journalistic media, as they combine to advance a particular variant of capitalist economic and social management. At other times, such as the current era of New Labour in power, good relations are more conditional, dependent on the pursuit of pro-business policies. With or without the economic support of big capital, however, political instruments for influencing the media are available to any political party once elected to government.

A third category of control mechanism, argue critical theorists of the dominance school, is *cultural*. Although much less true than it was a few years ago, it is still the case that many journalists, particularly those who reach the top of their profession, are recruited from a relatively narrow and privileged sector of society, where they have been reared to accept as 'natural', or as given, certain value systems and ideological positions which favour the dominant groups in society (that is, elites in the economic, political and cultural spheres) – groups to which they themselves may belong, or wish to belong. Others learn these values in the course of their professionalisation and enculturation (see Chapter 4). Either way, these values and ideas structure their ways of seeing and reporting the world – their *interpretive frameworks*. Ideology, in this sense, is present in journalism as part of the environment within which it is made. Journalism itself contributes substantially to the maintenance and reproduction of that environment and the social system which has generated it.

Because capitalist societies are hierarchical, it is argued, stratified along lines of class, gender and ethnicity to name but three important criteria of socio-economic status, ideology has to explain – make legitimate – inequality, and prevent the social tensions which it causes erupting into conflict. When, in the past, ideology has failed to do this, revolutions have resulted, and one ideology has taken the place of another (Marxism–Leninism in early twentieth-century Russia, for example, or Islamic fundamentalism in late twentieth-century Iran).[5]

A successful ideology has therefore to *explain* and make sense of the world – as it looks from the point of view of those who are at the top of the hierarchy – to those who are less advantaged, for it is the latter who are likely to have the greatest problems with inequality and injustice. In terms of critical theory, dominant groups use ideology as one means – the most important means in modern liberal democracies where military suppression of dissent is generally frowned upon – of securing and perpetuating their privileged positions. Ideology both reflects the prevailing system of social stratification and tries to justify it. Patriarchal ideology, for example, has advanced many reasons for the differentiated social statuses of men and women. In earlier, less enlightened times social and ethnic inequality was rationalised in relation to all manner of pseudo-scientific, quasi-religious notions.

Since the emergence of a critical sociology of journalism in the 1960s it has been driven by the dominance paradigm, with its presumption of a social world characterised by relations of exploitation, into which categories such as class, sex and ethnicity are placed: the ruling class over the workers; men over women; white over black. In all cases advocates of the dominance paradigm argue that those who staff the journalistic media are more or less committed, more or less direct promoters of these hierarchies, articulating and disseminating dominant values as the prerequisite for the survival of systems of material, structural inequalities. From the content analytical work of the Glasgow University Media Group (GUMG) in the 1970s, through the writings of Stuart Hall and his colleagues at the Birmingham Centre for Contemporary Cultural Studies (CCCS), to the most recent discourse analyses, the sociology of journalism has consisted largely of efforts to theorise about and/or demonstrate empirically how journalists carry out these functions in practice;[6] to show how, as John Fiske puts it, 'the media . . . structure the range of public voices in a hierarchy of legitimation that is a product of the dominant value system' (1996, p. 188). These approaches have been consistently critical of the liberal pluralist framework, and the competitive paradigm which underpins it, denouncing these as themselves part of the dominant ideology of capitalism, rhetorics of legitimation which mask the biases inherent to journalism in a stratified society.

The paradigm case, as it were, of the dominance paradigm concerns class, and was first systematically articulated by Karl Marx in the mid-nineteenth century when he set out his theory of historical materialism, which included the rudiments (though he never developed the theory fully) of an influential theory of the role of culture within capitalist societies. Historical materialism, as expressed by Marx, Friedrich Engels and the tradition of critical sociology which they founded, hypothesised a direct link between the economic structure of a society and its cultural life. To quote from Marx and Engels's *German Ideology*, 'the class which has the means of material production at its disposal also controls the means of mental production' (1976, p. 59). By doing so the dominant economic class – 'the ruling *material* force of society' – also becomes the dominant intellectual, cultural force. Its material domination is reflected in intellectual domination. For materialism, indeed, the latter is a precondition of the former. Although coercion has been, and on occasion continues to be employed as a means of maintaining the subordination of the economically and thus socially disadvantaged in society, persuasion is usually the preferred means of control. In the materialist model, subordinate social groups (classes) consent at some level to the system of stratification in which they find themselves. They internalise the dominant value system (ideology) as it is articulated in the culture around them, adopting it as a code for the organisation of their lives even when the effect of that internalisation is to perpetuate the domination of the wealthy and the powerful over them.

Sociologists since Marx and Engels have laboured to understand the means by which intellectual order is maintained in the interests of the ruling classes and how potential threats to that order have been contained. Early in the twentieth century the Italian Antonio Gramsci proposed a theory of *hegemonic class rule* in which the values of the dominant economic groups spread through society by means of the family, church and educational and media institutions, coming to be accepted as being for the general good. French philosopher Louis Althusser proposed a theory of *ideological interpellation*,[7] which borrowed heavily from Freudian psychoanalysis to suggest that media texts moulded their audiences' subconscious minds, turning them into the manipulable subjects of the capitalist order. The form and content of the message, he suggested – its very structure – compelled a response from the reader/viewer which was beyond his or her capacity to resist. Media, including journalism, 'produced the bourgeois subject' in the process of message construction and reception. Althusser's theory was influential in the 1970s and early 1980s, but his intellectual credibility, and indeed, his sanity were thrown into question when he murdered his wife and then announced from prison his conversion to Catholicism.

In the United States Noam Chomsky and Ed Herman have championed a more direct approach to the theorisation of journalism's place in capitalistic culture, arguing since the 1970s for a 'propaganda model' in which a C. Wright Millsian power elite conspires to control the news and information agenda and to suppress or marginalise all threats to the established order. From backgrounds in linguistics and economics, respectively, Noam Chomsky and Ed Herman have elaborated what is in North American terms a distinctively radical left-of-centre materialist sociology, arguing that the journalistic media work more or less directly in the service of the ruling classes of Western society. Their 'propaganda model' asserts that the media are part of the 'National Security State' – effectively part of a committee of political, economic, military and cultural elites which by various mechanisms subordinates the media to its own interests and controls information flows:

> The media serve the interests of state and corporate power, which are closely linked, framing their reporting and analysis in a manner supportive of established privilege and limiting debate and discussion accordingly . . . The mainstream media not only allow the agendas of news to be bent in accordance with state

demands and criteria of utility, they also accept the presuppositions of the state without question. (Chomsky, 1989, p. 5)

Chomsky and Herman attempt to prove these and similarly straightforward assertions of conspiratorial intent in a number of meticulously researched but highly readable books, to which the interested reader is enthusiastically directed.[8]

Towards a new sociology of journalism: beyond the competition–dominance dichotomy

Although both the competitive and dominance models still have many influential adherents and continue in their opposition to define the parameters of academic and professional debate, neither is any longer adequate (if either ever was) in accounting for the complex realities of postmodern capitalism. On the one hand, the competitive–normative ideal of the fourth estate is fundamentally compromised by the realities of media ownership and control (see Chapter 6) and the uses to which that ownership and control is put. But the dominance–critical paradigm is hardly a more accurate model. Capitalism has self-evidently been more successful economically, and at less cost to social cohesion, than Marx predicted in the nineteenth century. (I restrict these remarks, of course, to the advanced capitalist societies. The capitalism described by Marx, with its child labour, gross exploitation and below-subsistence wages, still exists in the greater part of the underdeveloped and developing worlds.) Its political structure has at the same time tended to become more open and democratic as, after many decades of struggle by those hitherto excluded from citizenship rights, universal suffrage has been established in the course of the twentieth century (as recently as 1994 in South Africa) as the minimum acceptable norm for all liberal capitalist countries. This has major implications for the way we understand the exercise of power in such societies.

Historically, the dominant economic groups in society (what Marx and the materialist sociologists influenced by him have called 'the ruling classes') monopolised the means of ideological production through their control of the church and the limited media available to them. Until the invention of printing the absence of print media which could challenge their domination (and the fact of mass illiteracy) inhibited the development of alternative ideas. Until relatively recently, therefore, the possibilities of critical, subversive media commentary were, for technological and political reasons, minimal. In the course of the twentieth century, however, dominant economic groups lost much of their power to monopolise the means of intellectual production. Newspapers and broadcast media are, as a rule, still the property of a very few rich men (or of corporations started by rich men and now owned by conglomerations of rich men), but the content of these media is now so diverse and multisourced (for reasons to be explored below) that no ideology can be truly 'dominant' for any length of time if it does not correspond on some level to what ordinary people feel to be, and experience as, true. No account of events stands unchallenged any more. In the millenial age the media function not always or necessarily as a tool of ideological domination (although this may be their function in some cases) but often as an arena for a real (as opposed to tokenistic or illusory) competition of ideas and interpretations of events.

The expansion of media channels, and the proliferation of the journalistic media in particular, has tended to erode the cultural and ideological power of elite groups in advanced capitalist societies. The modern journalistic media have become, over time, and particularly in the 1990s, less closed to views other than those which are at any given time 'dominant'; they are more open and accessible to the pluralism of views idealised by liberal theory than ever before. Socioeconomic hierarchies remain, but their structures change, and the struggle between competing ideologies and belief systems, fuelled by increasing flows of information, continually intensifies.

At any given time, of course, with the exception of periods of revolutionary change such as occurred in Eastern Europe after 1989 or in South Africa after 1994, there is still media-fuelled consensus around key values, but no group can assume that economic or political power guarantees ideological domination or that any idea is not subject to regular and vigorous challenge from the multiplicity of journalistic channels existing in the media marketplace.

In this sense, it is clear that the twentieth-century proliferation of journalistic media – and the formal, stylistic and editorial diversity which has characterised their development at the end of that century – has been a force not only for ideological control but also and increasingly for democratisation, facilitating and encouraging the emergence of genuine mass political participation from the empty shell of bourgeois democracy which Marx, Lenin and others so vigorously and justifiably condemned as a sham in the previous century. The speed and quantity of contemporary information flow, and its accessability to mass publics, threatens elite power at its core. What US President J. F. Kennedy could get away with, President Bill Clinton must publicly confront.

At the same time as individual members of elites have become more exposed to journalistic scrutiny, governmental decision-making has had to become more accountable and responsive, simply because it is more widely and rapidly reported than ever before. The once confidential and secret information on which decision-makers act is now increasingly *public* property, transmitted by the media around the globe at the speed of light. This threatens the very foundations of political control (whether with negative or positive social consequences I leave to the judgment of the reader) and reduces the potential for abuse of power by 'dominant' groups. Instead of ruling class ideological control, in the 1990s we have *mass cultural information chaos*.

All of this is complicated by the fact (not in itself new, since Marx was well aware that individual capitalists were locked in fierce competition with each other)[9] that although we can identify a dominant economic class in the abstract, materialist sense (a relatively small group of individuals defined by their ownership and control of the means of capitalist production) it rarely acts as a coherent political force. Because of mass education and social mobility the contemporary 'ruling class' is becoming ever more culturally diverse and, because of its different economic interests (manufacturing, financial and communication capital may all have different priorities at any given time) often divided in political terms, as revealed by the split over European union within the British 'ruling class' (Rupert Murdoch opposes it, manufacturing capitalists welcome it, financiers do not much care as long as London retains its pre-eminence as a global financial trading centre). Intra-class fragmentation and lack of ideological unity lead to revolving political elites, within a range extending from left-of-centre social democracy to aggressive free-market capitalism.

This is a social environment in which, fuelled by the media, 'dominant' ideology develops in unpredictable and unexpected directions. Evolutionary biologist Richard Dawkins refers to *memes* (ideologies) and their evolution in *The Selfish Gene* (1989), making the point that, like biological clusters of genes, sets of ideas seem to prosper or die out according to their 'fitness' for survival in the prevailing social environment. The existence of the media, it is clear, has accelerated this process of ideological evolution.

In contemporary capitalism, for example, patriarchal ideology (once considered essential to the social reproduction of wage labour; see note 4) has declined and is dying out, as a result of the counter-vailing force of women's growing socio-economic power and the ideology which legitimises that power. Capitalism survives, indeed goes from strength to strength, but against a backdrop of consensual feminism in which women are in theory, if not yet in practice, the equals of men. How has feminist ideology become consensual in such a short time? The answer lies largely, if not solely, in its acceptance as 'common sense' by the institutions of the media and the people who work in them.

Racism, too, is a dying ideology in modern capitalism, redundant and outmoded where once it was a routine element of many 'respectable' citizens' world-views. There are still racists in advanced capitalist societies, of course, but they are increasingly isolated, finding no endorsement of their views from the 'dominant' ideology, or the media which are its carriers.

Even the prejudice (one would not wish to dignify it with the name 'ideology') we call homophobia is in retreat, as being gay and having the right to proclaim and celebrate one's gayness slowly but surely becomes part of mainstream culture in the Western world.

Adherence to the dominance paradigm, then, and the associated hypothesis that the media, and journalism in particular, perpetuate relations of exploitation and inequality within capitalism, implies a degree of conspiratorial intent, class/sex/ethnic-based unity and ideological stasis which conflicts with the experience of the late twentieth century.

What *can* be said with some confidence is that journalism is a disseminator of values as well as facts; that its narratives are built around assumptions which producers and consumers take for granted; that journalism is a moral and ideological force as well as a source of cognitive data. It is also true that liberal journalism is biased towards capitalism in general – as the form of economic, social and political organisation within which it was born and has developed – but not towards a rigid capitalism in which relations of dominance and subordination are forever fixed and unchanging. The founding theorists and political philosophers of capitalism, fearing a return to the despotisms of the feudal epoch, gave journalism an independent role. That independence is taken seriously and is the source of autonomous journalistic power.

Whether simplistic or complicated, rigid or flexible, twentieth-century attempts to formulate an all-embracing theory of ideological domination in which the media were inevitably central have failed to keep pace with these developments and the way in which capitalism has been able to reinvigorate and reproduce itself by providing ever-rising standards of living and quality of life for the wage-labouring classes.

The dominance paradigm, and therefore the sociology of journalism based on it, has thus come under strain in recent years, not because there are no longer dominant and subordinate groups in society, nor value systems and ideologies which reflect the interests of competing social groups, but because these groups, values and ideologies no longer inhabit, if they ever did, the static positions suggested by traditional models. Marx himself never fully developed a theory of ideology to explain the mechanisms by which dominant economic forces realised their intellectual and cultural domination. Even if he had, the capitalism on which he based his work has changed, shifting its emphasis – at least in the advanced capitalist world – from production to consumption, from the brutal accumulation of profit to the maintenance of mass affluence and political consensus and, in the cultural sphere, from modernism to postmodernism, meaning in this context a media environment characterised by knowing, literate audiences familiar with, and resistant to, many of the codes of media production, including those of the journalist. These developments require a new sociology of culture and, within that, a new sociology of journalism. Sociology is not a predictive science, of course, nor one in which precise laws of motion can be discovered. Sociologists have no laboratories in which to conduct experiments, and must study living systems of which they are themselves a part. But sociology cannot evade the responsibility to explain and account credibly for the social phenomena which are its subject-matter, even if in an ultimately unprovable way. The sociology of journalism, dominated as it has been by the dominance paradigm, has not done so, and has now entered a necessary period of rethinking its key concepts and models.

Conclusions

Insofar as it addresses theoretical issues this book tries to reflect and engage with some of those uncertainties. It assumes that a more productive approach to the sociology of journalism is to break away from the competition–dominance, normative–critical, materialism–liberalism frameworks, focusing instead on the dynamics of the production environment and the relative impact of the elements within that environment on the form and content of output. The strength and influence of these elements, it will be shown in subsequent chapters, changes over time and according to institutional and other circumstances, and can be challenged, moderated or accentuated by journalists and other actors in the process. Their impact on content can be empirically studied (and recommendations made, should journalists and others wish to respond to them). The sociologist's task in confronting this environment is to map its contours, to make forecasts, where possible, about how particular events will be reported and to evaluate the likely consequences of that reportage on the wider social environment.

In the model used in this book the categories of dominance and subordination, exercised through economic and political power and leading to such features of content as 'ideological bias', still have a significant role in the sociology of journalism, but only as tendencies to prefer some accounts of events, some interpretations of the facts, over others. There are always other, opposing tendencies, other accounts and other interpretations existing in the *meme-pool*, which may negate and balance out a given tendency toward bias. The ideological role of the journalistic media, in this *chaotic flow* model as I will call it, becomes that of disseminating and articulating values and ideas which may *aspire* to and struggle for dominance but will not necessarily achieve it. The processes by which ideological dominance is achieved (or resisted and undermined) are random and unpredictable rather than systematised and hierarchically ordered. As with the elements of journalistic production discussed below, however, they can be empirically observed and analysed. In the process, they are rendered visible and opened to democratic scrutiny.

|3|

The effects of journalism

Although they differ in their assumptions and sociological implications, the perspectives reviewed in the previous chapter all start from the assertion that journalism is an important element in the cultural life of contemporary capitalist societies, a view shared by this writer. Journalism matters, economically and sociologically.

If this statement on its own would probably meet with broad agreement wherever journalism is produced and consumed, less straightforward is the precise characterisation of journalism's effects, both on the individuals who make up its audiences and on the social formations through which it circulates. The question posed in this chapter is not, therefore, 'Does journalism have effects?', but, 'What *kinds* of effects, impacts and influences does journalism have on individuals, organisations and social processes?'

Effects on individuals

To begin with the simplest, most direct relationship – that between the individual member of the audience and the journalistic text – journalism is a key element in shaping the cognitive environment within which we all live, which is simply to say that we think and act on the basis of what we believe to be true. Journalism is an important (though by no means the only) source of what we (think we) know about the world, so of course it affects us. In what it tells us, and in what it leaves out, journalism defines our field of socio-political vision. In this sense, journalism has very clear cognitive effects. Assuming that it commands our trust (and this is the key assumption when discussing the effects of journalism), we are willing to learn from it about the world we live in.

The next question is: does this learning affect our attitudes, ideas, values and patterns of behaviour? This is perhaps the wrong way to put the question. As psychologist Dorothy Rowe has written, 'The news we see on television and read in the papers has no effect on us whatsoever. What we are affected by is not the news but our interpretation of the news.'[1] Rowe does not mean by this that news is without effects but that the effects of journalism cannot be meaningfully discussed in relation to content alone. First, we have to understand how the content of a news text is perceived and interpreted by its audience – a mass of people who may number many millions, each with her or his own mix of pre-existing knowledges, views and dispositions which together will shape the meaning of the message and thus its consequences for attitude and behaviour.

Communication theory long ago came to terms with the fact that messages, on their own, cannot be said to have fixed meanings which are unproblematically injected into the minds of the audience as if through an ideological hypodermic. The hypodermic model of media effects, which dominated the field of communications theory until the 1950s, has been superseded by a more fluid approach, drawing on semiology and phenomenology, which stresses the *polysemic* (that is, containing many meanings) potential of all encoded media texts and the relative freedom of the audience in decoding those texts.

This hypothetical freedom of interpretation means that media effects can only begin to be understood (far less predicted!) when we know the nature of the reception environment into which messages are 'injected'. Without such knowledge statements about the effects of journalism (or any other form of media output) are strictly limited in their usefulness.

A model of journalistic effects

The individual's interpretation of a media text (and thus its *effect* on her or him at some point further down the causative chain of thought, behaviour and social consequence) is a factor of many different variables (Figure 3.1). Of overriding importance is the *cultural status* of the message, since it is this factor which cues the receiver to a particular kind of response. Debates about media effects in general often suffer from a failure to acknowledge this elementary point. Thus, those who warn of the danger of violent images in feature films may cite the power of advertising: if good advertising can persuade

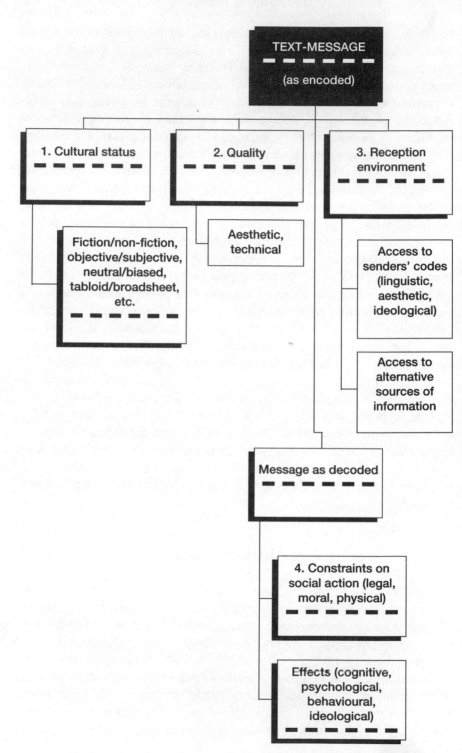

Figure 3.1 The effects of journalism: a four-step model

us to buy goods and services, cannot a film director glamorise violence with the effect of encouraging real-life imitation of the fictional acts depicted? This argument is appealing in its superficial obviousness, and thus frequently made by those who would be our moral guardians. But it wrongly conflates two quite different categories of phenomena.

An advertisement, on the one hand, is an appeal to action: its status as commercial propaganda is recognised by the audience (just as a political advertisement is recognised as ideological propaganda). Advertisements 'work' by alerting their audiences to the existence of a new product, or distinguishing one product from another in a crowded marketplace, in pursuit of a behaviour – consumption – which is highly valued in capitalist societies as an index of wealth and status. Advertisements seek to influence and facilitate the purchasing decisions of consumers by communicating information about the use, price and (often) style of the products they depict, referring to the range of social meanings in circulation at any given time. Those affected by being persuaded to buy are already 'in the market' for that category of product, or predisposed to be (I need, or think I need, a new car, and, assuming I have access to the necessary economic resources, am open to be persuaded that model A or B would be suitable). They recognise the 'committed' nature of the advertising, make their judgment and then their purchase.

Feature films, by contrast, are presented to the audience as fictions – imaginative narratives of a comedic, tragic or tragicomedic nature, depicting behaviours such as sex and violence in a wide variety of contexts. Rarely, if ever, do they exhort their audiences to imitate the behaviours depicted, although some sociopaths may use film images to inspire and script their own antisocial acts, just as respected books such as the *Bible* and Salinger's *Catcher In the Rye* have been implicated in notorious murder cases. For the vast majority of psychologically healthy individuals, however, the social barriers to committing acts of violence make it extremely unlikely that they will be influenced to do so by a Tarantino or Scorsese film. Conversely, those for whom society's ethico-moral rules do not apply rarely need a film to inspire their antisocial behaviour.

The meaning of an advertisement, in short, like that of a feature film, is inseparable from its semiological status – its *meaning*. The violence in a film 'means' something only in context – it may be intended to provoke revulsion and horror amongst its viewers for the purpose of entertainment (*Halloween*, John Carpenter, 1976). It may aim to induce critical reflection on the state of society (*La Haine*, Mathieu Kassovitz, 1995). Or it may aspire to be a satirical commentary on the journalistic media's fascination with violence (*Natural Born Killers*, Oliver Stone, 1994).

Which of these meanings attaches to a particular text (and there are many others we could identify) determines in part its interpretation by the individual in the audience and thence its translation into beliefs and social action.

The cultural status of journalism

In contrast to the messages contained in advertising or cinema, journalism is an account of mediated *reality*. As I suggested in Chapter 1, journalism claims to tell us something which is true about the world, even if that truth is acknowledged to be mediated by the subjectivity of the journalist, the constraints imposed by deadlines or one of the many other factors which journalists routinely mention when defending the limitations of their work. John Fiske puts it like this: 'The conventions of mainstream news . . . work to produce a believing subject who accepts that truth exists outside the conditions of its production, and can thus be known by a process of mere revelation (often called reporting)' (1996, p. 271). To put it another way: insofar as the conventions which signify 'believability' in journalism are present to our satisfaction (Chapter 4 describes what these conventions are in detail) we trust the journalist to represent the truth about the world to us. To that extent, too, the journalistic text may influence the way we see the world or that aspect of the world which it addresses.

The cultural status of journalism is, however, a variable quantity. Some journalistic messages are socially recognised to be truer than others. There is a semiological hierarchy of journalistic believability, going from television news (the most believable, for technical and culturo-historical reasons) to the most subjective, opinionated and inaccurate forms of print journalism, exemplified by the output of the *National Enquirer* in the United States and the *Daily Sport* in Britain. A little 'truer' than these, but still less true than television news or broadsheet newspapers, for example, are tabloid editorials (perhaps the most aggressively opinionated of mainstream journalistic forms). Newspapers in general, both tabloid and broadsheet, parade their editorial biases, but still make claims to some kind of truth, which their readers tend to accept.

The 'new journalism' movement, which came to prominence in the United States in the 1960s, intentionally set out to subvert the cultural status of journalism by combining it with the aesthetic conventions of literature and to highlight the fact that all supposedly objective accounts of reality are to some extent fictions. Partly because of the demystificatory work of the 'new journalists' we are in the 1990s, at this stage in our communicative evolution, perhaps less likely to accept journalism's claims than ever before. Audiences today are media literate, relatively suspicious and disbelieving and increasingly cynical. Informed scepticism about what is read, seen and heard in the journalistic media can be assumed to be a common feature of the contemporary reception environment. This puts pressure on journalists to work harder in convincing their audiences that, despite all of the cynicism-inducing events of the twentieth century, journalism is still privileged as a uniquely truthful source of knowledge.

The quality of information

In this sense, the quality of journalism is important in determining how it is interpreted and thus what its effects will be. The message, and its status as believable, credible information, has to get through, which it does through the adherence of its makers to certain technical and aesthetic standards. The elegance of a columnist's writing, the depth of a feature writer's research, the eloquence of a television news presenter's address, the interrogatory skill of an interviewer – these all play their part in communicating the message effectively. All assume technical proficiency sufficient to avoid the audience being distracted from the message content of what is being communicated, and adherence to those stylistic conventions which, as Deborah Cameron puts it, 'play[s] a role in constructing a relationship with a specific imagined audience, and also in sustaining a particular ideology of news reporting' (1996, p. 316).

The reception environment

Given that the source of a journalistic message is trusted, then, and that its intended meaning is communicated efficiently, the key remaining factor in determining its interpretation is the nature of the reception environment into which it is sent – the *decoding* or interpretive moment of the encoding/decoding process.[2]

Access to senders' codes

Of primary importance in determining interpretations of the journalistic message is the degree of audience access to the codes of the producers: and here we may include codes of both a linguistic and an ideological character. Clearly, the audience must understand the language in which a message is encoded, and in the vast majority of cases – given the existence of a specific linguistic community – will do so. On the other hand, even within that community the ability to deploy vocabulary will vary considerably, a fact which the journalistic market reflects in the differences of linguistic register and style which can be found, for example, in tabloid and broadsheet newspapers. Journalists are required, in this sense, to know their audience and to address its members with an appropriate level of linguistic complexity and sophistication. If the message is linguistically too simplistic or too difficult for its audience it will not get through successfully.

As was noted in Chapter 1, journalistic messages (like all narratives) are also coded *ideologically*, in the sense that they communicate values as well as facts, frameworks of interpretation as well as information. These values and frameworks are often unspoken, implicit rather than explicit in the text, presuming a shared culture or political identity which may not necessarily exist. If the ideological code applied by the receiver does not correspond with that of the producer/encoder of the message there will be difficulties in the transmission of shared meaning. For example, British media coverage of Sinn Fein leader Gerry Adams's historic (because first) visit to the prime minister's official residence on December 12 1997 (Figure 3.2) was structured by a variety of interpretive frameworks, most of them condemnatory insofar as they drew attention to the contradiction between the visit and his organisation's history of support for terrorist acts against, among others, the British government. To many British readers this coverage conveyed a 'truth' about the curious and often confusing development of the Northern Irish conflict in which the exchange of mortars in one period can be replaced by the exchange of diplomatic pleasantries in another. The effect of the coverage on such readers would likely have varied from incredulity, to anger, to pleasure, to cynicism. Some may have welcomed the meeting as an overdue concession from the British government, whereas others may have regarded it as a sign of Prime Minister Blair's weakness in the face of terrorism.

Figure 3.2 Sinn Fein go to Downing Street, December 1997

To Adams's mainstream Republican supporters in Belfast, on the other hand, the generally condemnatory interpretive framework of the United Kingdom press would likely have been ignored in preference for an alternative 'truth' or reading – the success of Adams's so-called 'bombs and ballot box' strategy in at last securing diplomatic recognition for their cause. For these readers, Adams's and his colleagues' presence on the front pages, albeit as hate figures, would have been the most important element of the story, one hypothetical effect of which may have been to strengthen their resolve.

Dissident Republicans, finally, who believe in no compromise with the British state, could well have interpreted the coverage as evidence for their belief in an impending 'sell out' of the cause by the Adams leadership.

From one story, then, comes many different meanings and as many potential effects on the attitudes and behaviours of diverse groups within the audience. This is the essence of Rowe's point.

Availability of alternative information

Beyond the need for understanding and acceptance by the receivers of the senders' codes, the main variables shaping the reception environment include the extent of an audience member's background knowledge of the story being told by the journalist. In short, does he or she know anything, independently of the journalist's account, about the events and issues being reported? If the answer to that question is 'yes' then the individual's interpretation of the journalist's message will be mediated by other information which may confirm or contradict it.

The extent of this knowledge depends, in turn, on the availability to the audience of alternative sources of information such as other journalistic media, word-of-mouth and anecdote gained from routine social interaction with family, peers, work colleagues and so on as well as actual experience of the events being reported. During the 1984–85 miners' strike, when British news media were filled with dramatic images of industrial conflict depicting aggression and violence coming from the workers involved, individuals who actually took part in the events, or who knew people who did, found the media images to be in sharp contrast to their own experiences, undermining their trust in mainstream journalism as the source of truthful accounts of reality. Conflict and violence emanating from the miners were felt by these groups to be exaggerated in journalistic accounts whereas that of the authorities was downplayed. Journalists' accounts conflicted with those readers' own experiences and memories of what had happened and thus lacked credibility. While the British people as a whole may have gained a negative impression of what the miners' strike was about from news coverage – because they trusted the news and had no alternative source of information about the dispute available to them – a significant proportion of the audience would not have interpreted the coverage in that way. Its 'effect' on them would thus have been very different.[3]

The extent to which journalism produces 'a believing subject' is, then, dependent on many things, not least the extent to which we apply our critical faculties to its output. Tired, lazy or uneducated audiences – couch potatoes (and we all tend to fall into that category from time to time) – may find themselves being seduced by the smooth glossy tones of the television news anchors, the seamless editing and the hi-tech newsgathering, until they forget that what they are getting is just as much a construction as the rants and diatribes of a tabloid newspaper columnist. On the other hand, alert, resourceful and educated audiences are quite capable of adopting, negotiating or rejecting the interpretive frameworks of the journalistic messages they read, see and hear. The news producer cannot predict in advance how the message will be interpreted, and the sociologist cannot predict what its effects will be. In general terms, however, we *can* say that the more trusted is the source of a message, the more efficiently its content is communicated, and the fewer alternative sources of potentially contradictory information there are available to the receiver the more powerful and effective a given journalistic message will be, other things remaining equal.

Constraints on action

The fourth and final element of our model relates to the problems associated with establishing a connection between belief and social action. There is, obviously, a connection of some kind, but what it is, exactly, is usually difficult, if not impossible, to describe. In some cases, such as the news coverage of the Ethiopian famine in 1984, knowledge generates mass action in a relatively unambiguous way. Then, journalistic information about a tragic and avoidable human catastrophe led to millions throughout the world making spontaneous financial donations to aid agencies (*before* Live Aid was organised), and there have been many other instances of news stories prompting similarly philanthropic actions on the part of individual audience members, whether prompted to or not by the reporting journalists. In such cases, the actions caused by journalistically originated information (its effects) are socially approved and may be assumed to confer prestige and self-esteem on the individual.

In some cases, such as the reporting of a food poisoning story, millions may choose not to buy a particular product because the news has made them fearful of the consequences, and may contain a warning not to purchase (see below). Here again, the link between information, belief and behaviour can be traced without too much difficulty.

In other cases, however, the cause–effect chain is less readily traceable. News about politics, for example, rarely produces obvious short-term or direct effects on voting behaviour (at least not of the kind that might be expected). Years of coverage of President Clinton's alleged financial and sexual peccadilloes did not prevent him winning a second term in 1996 (nor achieving record high popularity ratings in the United States one week after the breaking of the Monica Lewinsky scandal in January 1998). On the other hand, years of 'sleaze' coverage of the British Conservatives did, most observers agree, fatally damage their chances of winning the 1997 general election. Journalistic accounts of sleaze – which both in the United States and in the United Kingdom were largely media-generated stories, since the behaviours of Clinton, Merchant, Cook *et al.* were not necessarily qualitatively worse than those of their predecessors in history – did not have similar effects in both countries, because the political and moral environments within which they circulated were very different.

Similarly, news about social injustice sometimes produces riots in the streets, as in the Los Angeles riots of 1994, but in most cases does not. Individuals are aware of, and usually respect, social and legal constraints on their responses to the information obtained through journalistic media. Just as a viewer of Quentin Tarantino's *Reservoir Dogs*, will in all probability refrain from responding to it by cutting off a policeman's ear (an unlikely effect, if not theoretically impossible), doing so for reasons of social convention and self-preservation, the consumer of news will have many good reasons for not acting as his or her feelings about a particular story suggest he or she should or could act.[4]

All of this leads to the disappointing conclusion that we cannot predict merely by analysing the content of a journalistic message how important it is as a source of information for the receiver, how it will be decoded or how its interpretation will be translated into ideas and action. We may be able to identify, through content analysis or other means of establishing intention, the message-sender's *preferred* reading (that is, what the journalist wants to communicate) but we cannot infer from this the actual message received, since this depends on the individual's interpretation, and each interpretation is a highly individual thing, shaped not just by personal and psychological factors but also by assessments of the wider social environment.

At the risk of oversimplification, the following equation expresses the problem of effects in terms which, though they cannot be specified precisely, describe the likelihood of any particular message having consequences on the thoughts and behaviours of a receiver. As we can see, in general, the effect, E, of a journalistic text (defined as measurable physical or psychological change in the individual audience member) is proportional to the level of trust, T, which it inspires, the quality of its construction and delivery, Q, and the extent of shared understandings between sender and receiver, C. It is disproportionate to the number of alternative sources of information available to the audience, A, and to the extent of social disapproval or stigma attached to the implied effect, S:

$$E = \frac{T \text{ (trust)} + Q \text{ (quality)} + C \text{ ('sharedness' of codes)}}{A \text{ (availability of alternative information)} + S \text{ (stigma)}}$$

There is a large, possibly infinite, number of possible impacts of any given journalistic message (E). The environment into which it passes is characterised by constant variability and uncertainty. Journalism is one element in that environment, and often a highly visible, highly consequential element, but looking for its effects on individual thought and behaviour in specific cases is a frustrating endeavour, unlikely to yield satisfactory empirical results. This *does not* mean that the effects do not exist, simply that they cannot be measured or isolated from the effects of other environmental stimuli.

Having made this general statement, the rest of this chapter contains an examination of particular *types* of effect as they have been hypothesised and discussed in the sociological literature.

Ideological effects

As we saw in Chapters 1 and 2, journalists are communicators of *values* as well as of facts. They are key workers in the cultural apparatus which binds a society together, giving it ideological coherence and some degree of commonality or shared experience. They connect the individual to the social, the near to the faraway, the private to the public.

As Chapter 2 then showed, this role can be viewed as a socially necessary feature of the organisation of any complex society. The journalist is then positioned either as a benign force for diversity and pluralism (the normative–competitive paradigm), or as part of an oppressive mechanism for perpetuating exploitative social relationships (the critical–dominance paradigm). Journalistic media may also be viewed as an arena for ongoing ideological struggle, and the expression, in journalistic form, of the continually evolving 'dominant ideology' of a society.

Is it possible, then, to identify and measure specific ideological effects associated with journalism (apart from the dissemination of ideology in general) and to assess these effects in relation to the interests of 'dominant groups'?

John Fiske argues that journalism can affect what he calls the 'structures of feeling' existing in a society. In the United States, for example, coverage of the O.J. Simpson trial had a major impact on societal attitudes to ethnicity, sex and crime (Fiske, 1996), as did coverage of the Anita Hill hearings on the issue of sexual harassment. Fiske assesses these effects as negative (principally in their mobilisation of what he alleges to be racist stereotypes), but one could argue with equal force that they were positive. In the O.J. Simpson trial the US public witnessed through the medium of live television news the racism and incompetence of the Los Angeles Police Department being exposed to widespread outrage. This then became the basis of a black defendant's being acquitted (by a multi-ethnic jury) of murdering a white woman, despite what may be viewed as considerable evidence pointing to a contrary verdict. The Anita Hill trial, on the other hand, publicly demonstrated the seriousness with which the US politico-legal establishment must now take an issue that only a few years ago would have been marginalised as the obsession of feminist extremism.

In these cases US news media signalled the importance which they – and by implication US society – now attach to progressive race and gender politics and the extent to which they have incorporated once 'subordinate' discourses of antiracism and antisexism into mainstream news agendas. The Monica Lewinsky scandal also demonstrated this tendency, since it highlighted the issue of abuse of power by an older man over a younger (though adult and fully consenting) woman.

Although neat empirical evidence of this effect is unlikely to be available, it is easy to argue that journalists are both reflecting and affecting deep-rooted 'structures of feeling' about these issues among their audiences, replacing long-established traditions of racism and sexism with new consenses – that white policemen can indeed be viciously racist, that high-powered, successful career women can be the victims of harassment, that such stories are the appropriate stuff of primetime news.

In Britain the 1994 murder of Jamie Bulger and the trial of his killers was similarly era-defining, contributing to an already established public anxiety about the supposed decline of childhood innocence (the brutal killers were only children themselves), the failure of parental responsibility and the role of the media in producing increasingly violent young people. The 1996 mass murder of schoolchildren and their teacher in Dunblane had a similar impact. Journalists gave these stories prominence as news and at the same time unleashed painful public debates about the issues raised. The news media became a sounding board for the public to exorcise its feelings and, as Fiske suggests, perhaps even to change them. In these circumstances journalists may become a means of expressing the public mood in a society, or what is claimed to be the public mood. Tabloids often claim to 'speak' for the people in their banner headlines, editorials and commentary columns. By providing space for issues to be debated, and information and analysis on which to make judgments, they also seek to influence 'structures of feeling' and ultimately to affect real changes on policy-makers and governors.

For many observers, this journalistic 'demagogery' is damaging to liberal democratic societies in its effects, since it may lead to hastily drafted, ill-considered changes in the law. In the months following the Dunblane massacre, for example, and in the run up to Parliament's November 1996 vote on proposals to ban handguns in the United Kingdom, the *Sun* and other British tabloids mounted an intense pro-ban campaign in which the people's understandable disgust at the nature of the Dunblane crime was instrumental in manufacturing a climate where the Tory government and Labour opposition competed with each other to see who could crack down hardest on legal gunowners. In this case, development in the law was driven principally by press outrage and the perceptions of political actors in an election year that they had to be seen to be doing something. One does not have to feel solidarity with the hitherto law-abiding holders of small firearms to sense that the post-Dunblane coverage of the United Kingdom's gun law was about scapegoating and the exorcism of angst rather than rational policy development.

The death of Diana

A final example from the United Kingdom of these broad effects in practice was the media's coverage of the death of Princess Diana on 31 August 1997. In the immediate aftermath of the fatal car crash British broadcast organisations dispensed with their normal Sunday schedules and gave more or less blanket coverage to the incident. The press followed suit, and throughout the following week journalists in general treated the event as one of historic, epoch-making significance, rather than what, with a slightly more objective eye, it was – the tragic, untimely death of a by-then constitutionally minor, if still immensely popular, member of the British royal family. Unsurprisingly, millions of people responded to this cue and began exhibiting behaviour which the media had sanctioned and endorsed as appropriate in the circumstances. Entire families travelled hundreds of miles to stand for hours in the rain outside London's royal palaces. Normally detached republicans wept openly. Life-long socialists felt genuine grief for, and solidarity with, someone whom a few weeks before they would have denounced as an aristocratic, emotionally unstable multimillionaire.

And then, as the news media struggled for material to fill the space which they had made for the story, they turned on the other members of the royal family, opening a period of several days in which the future of the British monarchy was questioned as never before in recent history. The Windsors' characteristic and thus entirely predictable aloofness and icy detachment in dealing publicly with their bereavement were read by the media, and by the tabloids in particular, as evidence of spite and lack of concern for Diana. The popularity of the 'people's princess', as Prime Minister Tony Blair called her, was contrasted to the stiffness of the Queen and her advisors, who will have to deal for a long time to come with the long-term constitutional consequences of their actions that week in September 1997.

Much has already been written, and much more will be, about the complex relationship between the British people's 'structures of feeling' and the media's coverage of Diana's death. Did media coverage structure popular reaction to the death, giving legitimacy to the mass hysteria which accompanied it, as I have suggested, or did the media merely respond to a spontaneous outpouring of grief by millions of people, as the journalists themselves have argued in defence of their coverage? Both explanations are possible, since once the emotional floodgates were opened and national mourning had begun the media had only to report what was happening. There can, however, be little doubt that the impact of the event on the United Kingdom would have been very different had it not been for the manner in which it was defined by the media from the outset as a national crisis.

Public agenda-setting

Whether or not 'structures of feelings' are changed, we see in these examples how journalism can shape and define the environment within which events and issues are viewed as important, made available for public discussion then acted on. Journalism has the power to make things visible to the public and thus to make them important. 'The struggle for visibility', writes one journalist, 'is at the centre of all politics' (Woolacott, 1996). The power to make things visible is perhaps journalism's main 'effect' and one which, if we embrace its implications, allows the student to escape from the sterile debate about whether or not news has the power to shape thought and action like a hypodermic injection.

Events which are not reported have little or no social significance. They matter to those who are directly implicated in or affected by them, of course, but to no one else because no one else is aware of their existence. Journalism gives events social meaning and thus makes them real for the society as a whole, which is usually the prerequisite for organised social action. Our concerns about the world are not related so much to what is happening as to what journalists *tell us* is happening. This is a powerful effect with huge implications for wider social processes.

The 1988 bombing of a PanAm 747 over Lockerbie, Scotland, for example, was a highly visible event and the cause of an international political crisis with major consequences for Libya, accused of planting the device which brought the aircraft down. When, by contrast, an Air India 747 went down off the coast of Ireland, it too the probable victim of a terrorist bomb, the event had low visibility, and even less political significance for the Western news audience.

In 1984 British television news coverage of the Ethiopian famine caused an international wave of public concern, followed by an outburst of charitable giving and eventually government action. Famine was present in the area before 1984 but had not been reported, so it did not exist for the Western publics, who take their cue on the importance of events from what they read, see and hear in the news media. Iyengar and Kinder observe that

> By priming certain aspects of national [and international] life while ignoring others, [the] news sets the terms by which political judgments are rendered and political choices made . . . When the news focuses on a problem, the public's priorities are altered, and altered again as [it] moves on to something else.[5] (1987, p. 33)

This is potentially a much more productive way of thinking about journalism's impact than is looking for individually-located behavioural or ideological effects. The two approaches are in any case hard to separate, as Robert Entman observes:

> The distinction between 'what to think' and 'what to think about' is misleading. Nobody, no force, can ever successfully 'tell people what to think'. Short of sophisticated torture or 'brainwashing', no form of communication can compel anything other than feigned obeisance. The way to control attitude is to provide a partial selection of information for a person to think about, or process. The only means of influencing what people think is precisely to control what they think about. (1989, p. 77)

Few will doubt the validity of these assertions. They raise some interesting and important questions for research, however. Which media are the most important in setting the agenda – the press, television or radio? How do we measure agenda-setting effects? By topping the news agenda an event is, by definition, of high newsworthiness, but how does an event become so important? Are journalistic news values responding to some innate characteristic of the event, or are journalists simply fodder for the news management strategies of social actors seeking to make the news? In most cases a news agenda is the product of several factors, including professional criteria of news value (Chapter 4) and news management or 'source strategies' (Chapter 8). One of the tasks of the sociology of journalism is to understand how these factors make their influence felt in particular circumstances and to show that the journalistic process of making events visible is not value-free. It is, inevitably, selective, partial and vulnerable to bias. The picture journalism gives us of an event may not be – cannot be – the whole picture. The question then becomes, 'Whose picture, whose agenda, is it, and constructed from whose viewpoint?' We will return to this question in the analysis in Part II of the production process of journalism.

Moral panic and the amplification of problematic reality

The agenda-setting approach confers on journalism the important function of watchdog on the public's behalf: warning about dangers as they arise, facilitating discussion of the possible responses and representing public concern to the politicians. In many cases, however, the 'dangers' or problems exposed by news coverage turn out to have far less statistical significance than the quantity and quality of their coverage would suggest.

A variant of the agenda-setting approach asserts that the journalistic media play a role in defining as problems those phenomena which we – and which the forces of law and order in society – become concerned about. In this sense, news alerts us to the existence of *problematic reality* and thereby generates public anxiety which in turn generates an official response. The massacre at Dunblane, as we noted above, eventually produced a complete ban on civilian ownership of handguns in the United Kingdom. An earlier series of stories concerning dogs savaging children produced the Dangerous Dogs Act, prohibiting certain breeds and types of dog from being owned as pets or from being walked in public without muzzles.

In the 1970s sociologists such as Stan Cohen and Jock Young (1973) introduced the concept of *moral panic* into social theory, referring to a state of media-generated public anxiety about a phenomenon far in excess of what the incidence of that phenomenon would rationally justify. Moral panic, it was argued, was often translated into official action against the 'folk devils' or deviants responsible for the alleged problem – new laws and regulations, more stringent and authoritarian policing, harsher sentences – which then fed back into the media in a further wave of reportage and an intensification of the moral panic.

In the British case of dangerous dogs, for example, newspapers around the country reported an initial series of tragic incidents involving particular breeds (Rottweilers and pit bull terriers were especially prominent in coverage). The incidents were not statistically out of the normal range of attacks on humans by dogs, but the appearance of several superficially similar stories around the same time gave the impression of a 'wave' of such incidents. This 'wave' then became the basis for other, similar, stories being given enhanced newsworthiness, contributing to the emerging picture of a country overrun by vicious and out-of-control dogs. To the public, taking its cue from the journalistic agenda, dangerous dogs had become a major law-and-order issue.

The news media responded to this perception by reporting more and more dangerous-dog stories while at the same time calling on the authorities for action to deal with the problem. In the end, and to virtually unanimous support from public and parties, the Conservative Government introduced its Dangerous Dogs Act, outlawing certain breeds and placing severe restrictions on the ownership and care of others. Eventually, as editors exhausted the news angles and got bored with the story, it disappeared from the media and the panic died away (although the incidence of savaging by dogs of all kinds did not). The 'problem' of dangerous dogs went away as quickly as it had arrived in the public imagination, placed there by a media hungry for stories filled with drama, pathos and opportunities for righteous anger.

A similar phenomenon can be observed in public perceptions of crime. In Britain, media coverage of crime has traditionally focused on the dramatic and the relatively unusual transgressions – crimes of violence against children, women and elderly people. Although young single men are the most likely to be violently attacked, 'worthy victims' are more newsworthy and thus take up more space in the news media. As a consequence, public perceptions exaggerate the risk of events which are highly improbable (child murder, for example) and downplay crimes which are much more likely to happen to the average person. Women and elderly people live with a fear of being attacked which is agreed by police and criminologists to be out of all proportion to the chances of such an event happening. In this example the public's perceptions of crime – their anxieties, fears and panics – are argued to be the direct consequence of the prominence of certain categories of crime in the news media. Journalist Julie Flint, in a 1995 television documentary about perceptions of the risk of violent crime, argued that 'sensationalist [media] emphasis on isolated crimes encourages the myth that these are especially dangerous times for women. It isn't true. Young men are almost twice as likely to be attacked'.[6] Journalists, of course, are not deliberately stoking up such fears for malicious reasons. It is simply that, for a variety of reasons (including the need to sell papers and maximise ratings), some crimes are more attractive as news stories than others. By default, these stories and images then become part of the social reality which people accept as 'normality' and live with.

In recent years coverage of a succession of 'food panics' and health scares has provided illustration of the media's power to define and then amplify problematic social reality. Typically, in such cases an event which is extremely rare (statistically and in comparison with other events of a similar category) becomes defined by the media as a major threat to health. Consumers naturally stop buying the product, at least temporarily while the scare is on; government departments take emergency action to deal with the threat; sometimes, whole industries are decimated as their markets collapse overnight. In Britain this has been the pattern with eggs (the salmonella scare of the 1980s); cheese (listeria); and, most significantly, beef (bovine spongiform encephalopathy – BSE or 'mad cow disease'). The BSE scare of March 1996 caused immense damage to British agriculture despite the fact that by the beginning of 1998 less than 20 people were believed to have died from the human form of BSE, Creutzfeld–Jacob disease (CJD). In one average year in Britain, by comparison, some 3000 people die in road traffic accidents, 70 000 die from smoking-related diseases and 90 000 are killed by the effects of alcohol. Not only are the products which cause these deaths not banned but their use is actively promoted by a multibillion-dollar advertising industry.

In 1996 British public health authorities released to family doctors new guidelines concerning the prescribing of oral contraceptives. One particular version of 'the pill', it was tentatively suggested, might increase the risk of coronary thrombosis in some women and should therefore be used with caution. Although the relative risk associated with the new pill was significantly higher than with an earlier version of the medication (an increased risk factor of two was

indicated) the absolute risk was extremely low and certainly much
lower than the risk of thrombosis accepted by the average woman in
the course of a normal pregnancy. The story was leaked to the news
media, however, and before the level of risk could be clarified and put
into context thousands of British women stopped taking the new pill.
Hundreds of unwanted pregnancies, deaths from pregnancies, and
abortions were the inevitable outcome. In this case, disproportionate
media coverage of a relatively minor problem created a much more
serious one, with tragic consequences for many women.

Here, as in many other cases, perceptions of risk are almost entirely
unrelated to the actual incidence of a phenomenon in society, arising
instead from the visibility given to that phenomenon by journalists.

In panics of this sort journalism is not the only proactive force
involved but is a focus and a catalyst for social action. The journalists report the event and in doing so label it as a socially meaningful
issue – in most cases, a problem. Other journalists become sensitive
to similar stories, which are also reported, to give the impression of a
major and growing problem. Readers write in about the problem;
editorial columns pronounce on it; radio and television phone-ins
take place; politicians and law enforcers feel obliged to respond even
if they know that the degree of response demanded is out of
proportion to the risk.

As we see in such cases as the handgun and dangerous dog
debates, journalistic institutions have the power to encourage and
even force change on other institutions. Some of this power is intentionally and purposefully wielded; some is the consequence of the
growth of journalism as a cultural force. In the first case journalism
has a campaigning role, derived from its democratically ordained
function of scrutinising the powerful and protecting citizens from
abuse. Journalists can and do campaign for and against things which
they like or dislike, and their campaigns often succeed. Having set an
agenda, the media will only succeed in affecting change at the political level if the target organisation perceives that public opinion
demands change and that the costs of not responding are greater than
those of responding. This is a political calculation over which the
media have little direct control. What the journalists *can* do is to
maximise publicity and thus exert pressure, both in relation to the
initial wrongdoing and in highlighting public concern about the
'problem' (whether it really exists or not).

The mobilisation of society around hitherto neglected problems
can be one of the positive effects of journalism or, as in the case of

moral panics, it may be judged unhelpful to the sensible administration of society. Often, those labelled as 'folk devils' in moral panics suffer discrimination and harm as a result. In the early years of the human immunodeficiency virus (HIV) epidemic, carriers of the virus, and gay men in particular, experienced serious problems from publics who had learnt all they knew about the disease from sensationalist and ignorant reportage.[7] In the case of BSE, no one yet knows how dangerous to human beings the condition really is, and it will be some years before we know if the damage caused to the British beef industry, meat processors and retailers and others affected by the collapse in the market was justified or not.

I will conclude this section by noting that, as a rule, media scares should be treated with scepticism, balanced by an awareness that the conventions of newsmaking (see Chapter 4) and the desire for good stories tends to privilege the dramatic and the spectacular over the complex and dull, often at the expense of information accuracy.

Journalism and organisational effects

As the late-twentieth-century history of moral panics and food scares demonstrates, the journalistic media have become steadily more important as 'reality-defining' institutions. They have become synonymous with the public sphere – that intermediate zone between governors and the governed where public opinion is formed and reformed. The journalistic media are the main source of our information about politics and public affairs in general (what other sources do we have if we are not political activists?) as well as setting the agenda. Politicians and public organisations – social actors in general – have gradually come to understand this and to adapt their organisations and practices accordingly. To the extent that the perceived impact of the media on public opinion produces changes in the organisation of political and other institutions – changes designed to improve communication in various ways – we can speak of *organisational effects*.

Political actors, like others, cannot know with any precision what effect a particular piece of visual or verbal information has or will have on the audience (although modern marketing aspires to find out through focus-group and other research), but a gradual consensus has emerged that access to the media, on favourable terms, is a key element in successfully pursuing a political agenda. This is as true for pressure and lobby groups, business organisations and trade unions as it is for political parties. The media, and journalism in particular, have thus become the organisational focus for an increasing proportion of political activity (defined broadly to include non-party actors). This has had major consequences (effects) for the way political decisions are taken and presented, and although there is no space in this volume for a detailed analysis of contemporary political communication practice, they should at least be mentioned in a general discussion of media effects such as this (for a detailed analysis, see McNair, 1995).

Effects on political campaigning and promotion

As a consequence of the contemporary centrality of journalism in the formation of public opinion political actors have developed much more sophisticated and professional news management apparatuses designed to secure large quantities of favourable media coverage. 'Modern' political events, as we shall see in Chapter 8, are designed and directed like stage shows, with the news values of the journalists in mind.

Presentational aspects of policy have become much more important than ever before. Successful political action is assumed to be, at least in part, a function of favourable public opinion, in the securing of which the media's cooperation, if not necessarily support, are crucial. In all aspects of the modern political process a concern with how decisions and actions will be reported is central to the calculations of strategists and tacticians.

For many observers this aspect of journalism's effects is a negative one, associated with the trivialisation and 'dumbing down' of democratic political culture alleged by some to be a key trend of the late twentieth century. The widespread perception of the media's increased role in the political process has forced unwelcome adaptations upon the latter, which, it is argued, we should resist and reverse. Some, such as James Fallows (1996), editor of the US periodical *The Nation*, complain that the style and content of modern political debate has been distorted by the demands of the news media, who for reasons of their own favour confrontation over compromise, and conflict over consensus. Political journalists are argued to have become referees in gladiatorial contests fought out on air or in print between politicians desperate to be seen to be performing well by their audiences.

Others, including this writer, are less pessimistic about the negative impact of intensifying media coverage of politics, arguing that changes in the political process are an inevitable by-product of universal suffrage, mass media technology and growing political sophistication on the part of the audience. The expanded political media, as was suggested in Chapter 2, have weakened the authority of elites and enhanced democratic scrutiny over them. If this is an effect of political journalism then it should be welcomed.

The important point to emerge from this debate is the following: to the extent that we believe journalism to be important it *is* important and *does* have effects on individual and organisational perspectives of the world. The assumption that journalism has effects *produces* real, empirically observable effects on the communicative behaviour of individuals and organisations.

Conclusions

The cultural power of journalism – and any effects it may have – are rooted in its discursive status as 'truth'; its ability to mobilise belief and consent (actively or passively) through the telling of stories which are credible *because* they are journalistic. The producers of journalism cannot take this credibility for granted but must constantly assert and reassert their status through codes and conventions which signify 'truth' and 'believability' to the audience.

The cultural (ideological) power of journalism thus defined is what makes influencing it (and in democratic societies, influencing it without being seen to) important to those who would exercise political power. The ownership and control of print and broadcast journalistic media is presumed to bring with it power in the political sphere because underpinning the 'truth' of any successful journalistic account of events is a statement of values and ideology.

But the audience has power to resist or reject the message, to contextualise and interpret news in ways beyond the control of any journalist or spin doctor. Journalists carefully shape the content of their output in accordance with the demands of their editors, managers and proprietors; news managers and source professionals can seek to intervene in the process and to put a particular 'spin' on the story, but neither group can dictate how the story is interpreted by the audience nor what its effects on them will be. Unpredictability and chaos, rather than order and stability characterise the reception environment.

On that note of sociological uncertainty we can turn now to the description and analysis of the factors which contribute to the production of journalism, beginning with those which we can group together under the heading 'professional factors'.

PART

II

THE FACTORS OF JOURNALISTIC PRODUCTION

4

The professional culture and organisational determinants of journalism

Chapter 1 attempted, by way of introduction, to define what journalism is and what distinguishes it from other types of discourse. Chapter 2 examined the normative principles, roles and functions of journalism in liberal democracy and critically evaluated differing perspectives on how those principles and roles are applied in practice. Then, Chapter 3 discussed various ways of conceptualising the impact of journalism on society. With this background material in place we can now focus on the core subject matter of the sociology of journalism: the elements – historical, technological, political and economic – which are involved in its construction.

Most of those factors, to be explored in subsequent chapters, are experienced by the journalist as external forces acting on his or her work: pressures emanating from the demands, reasonable or unreasonable, of politicians and proprietors; pressures of the market in which the journalist's work must be packaged and sold and over which he or she has relatively little control; and pressures caused by the new technologies which continually impact on the production process. Underpinning all this, however, is the professional status of the journalist and the collective character of the work she or he does. The journalist is a professional communicator whose work is structured and shaped by a variety of practices, conventions and ethical norms as well as by the constraints and limitations imposed by the fact that journalism is a complex production process requiring sophisticated organisation. This chapter is concerned with the professional and organisational factors involved in the production of journalistic texts, based on the premise that news content is a product of the professional ethics, routine practices and bureaucratic organisation of journalists. These influences make themselves felt through the process of journalistic education in colleges and universities or are passed on in the workplace as taken-for-granted assumptions about how things are done. Either way, they represent a significant influence on the output of journalism. They are also the cause of certain features of contemporary journalism which are the subject of criticism. Bias, for example, may be, as we will see, the product of political or economic forces acting on the journalist. On the other hand, bias where it exists may be the outcome of routine professional practices which have the effect of skewing reportage in one direction or another. This chapter will show how and why this happens.

Bureaucratic and formal determinants of output

Before that, however, we might begin with the observation that journalism is, as a *social construction*, the result of a production process centred on the newsroom and that the working environment of the newsroom is the starting point for the individual journalist's activity, defining its routines and limitations. The journalist does what has to be done to produce the goods, within the constraints set by deadlines and competitive pressures. He or she is an employee, subordinate to a line management extending all the way up to the proprietor. This is, perhaps, an obvious point, but one worth making if only because much of what and how journalists produce is predetermined by these constraints. Those who criticise journalistic output, from a left-of-centre or a right-of-centre perspective, often overestimate the extent to which journalists are free agents and thus these critics may easily address their criticisms to the wrong location. The journalist is a cog in a wheel over whose speed and direction he or she may have little or no control, and the sociologist is obliged to acknowledge this fact, as indeed many important studies have (for example, see Schlesinger, 1987).

One illustration of how changes in the bureaucratic organisation of the newsroom affect content is the phenomenon of environmental news. In the early 1980s there was very little coverage of environmental issues in the mainstream media because the issue was still low on the international political agenda. As environmentalism increased its profile in the late 1980s, however – the product among other things of pressure group lobbying (see Chapter 8) – many newspapers began to have 'environmental correspondents'. Once established as a feature of the newsroom, environmental correspondents had to justify their existence and salaries by reporting the environment, leading to a significant and generally welcome increase in the attention given the environment by the media. The environment – more specifically, the process of environmental damage unleashed by global industrialisation, and its real and potential impact on human societies – became part of the news agenda.

Conversely, in Thatcher's Britain of the 1980s, as the unions came under economic and judicial attack and the power of organised labour was weakened and the number of industrial disputes fell, the once-important professional category of 'industrial correspondent' declined in visibility. 'Industrial news', which had dominated the news agenda in the 1970s (see GUMG, 1976) shrank as a proportion of total output, making the top of the agenda only in the context of major disputes such as the 1984–85 miners' strike. A similar fate befell the post of labour correspondent, and for similar reasons. Ralph Negrine observes that 'as the nature of the industrial landscape changed and the fortunes of the labour movement dramatically declined, the need for a labour correspondent all but disappeared' from most print and broadcast media (1996, p. 83).

In the cases of both environmental and industrial news, organisational changes in the newsroom, responding to perceived changes in the political environment beyond the newsroom, affected the way the world was broken down, categorised and translated into news. If journalism may be thought of as an *organised* response to events taking place in the world, changes in the social environment affect the way in which that organisation is structured.

Journalistic form

Journalistic work is heavily and obviously constrained by the formal requirements of the different media available. We consider the technology of news production in Chapter 7, and the formal implications of the application of objectivity below, but here it is worth noting that the various media of print, television and radio journalism each tend to prefer different modes of communication, utilising different properties of language. These have their relative advantages and disadvantages, which journalists must be aware of and be able to work around. Television news, for example, allows for and requires a strong visual component which, once found, tends to limit the words which are appropriate to use as accompaniment. Film of an ecstatic political rally, for example, with balloons, bunting and a smiling, waving politician, will tend to require a positive, upbeat commentary – 'writing to the picture', as journalists sometimes refer to it. Images of starving children in a third world famine zone will tend to impose another kind of narrative.

Radio, on the other hand, allows the journalist more freedom to 'fill in' the visual dimension of the story – which may be signified by a soundtrack – with elaborate verbal description, free of the distraction presented by pictures. Print journalism, of course, may employ all the literary tricks of reportage and fiction (see below), at much greater length than broadcast media can allow, to convey complex and sophisticated meanings which are beyond the capability of television and radio.

Journalists then, like artists, must know the strengths and weaknesses of their form and the media available for the dissemination of their texts and be able to exploit both. This knowledge is expressed in codes and conventions which act as formal disciplines and constraints.

The journalistic profession

For the sociologist, journalism, like any other form of cultural production, always reflects and embodies the historical processes within which it has developed and the contemporary social conditions within which it is made. Concepts such as objectivity and balance – so important to journalists in their everyday work – have complex socio-historical roots which reflect the values and ideas of the societies in which they emerged. In this sense, too, journalism is a social construction.

Journalism is also a profession, and as such it must have an ethical code. To be accepted as a professional group journalists (like doctors, lawyers and academics) must be seen to work to a code of conduct which guarantees their integrity, their trustworthiness and thus their status as reporters of 'truth'. Doctors of medicine produce a discourse of the body, which we must believe if we are to place our trust in their professional hands. Medical ethics (as codified in the

Hippocratic oath) are intended to sustain the belief of the rest of us in the validity of medical science. In the same way lawyers' ethics 'guarantee' their discourse of justice, legitimising legal work as honourable and dispassionate, even if it means defending a child murderer.

Academics also have ethical codes (no plagiarism, for example) which are intended to secure widespread faith in what they say about the phenomena they deal with. The rhetorical structure of the academic text, with its supporting apparatus of notes and references, and its often highly technical language ('jargon', in the popular vernacular), is a device for securing acceptance of what one writes from fellow professionals and students as much as facilitating the dissemination of knowledge.

The journalist's profession, as we have seen, might be described as that of 'authorised truthteller', or 'licensed relayer of facts'. Journalism is presented to its audience as a truthful discourse about the real world, and it must command legitimacy on these terms or it is without value in the cultural marketplace. Thus, journalistic ethics can be seen as a device to facilitate the social construction of legitimacy, to mobilise the trust of the audience in what they are reading, hearing or seeing. In their proclamation and definition ethical standards also – if they are taken seriously by practitioners – of course have a major impact on journalistic content.

Objectivity

The concept of objectivity is the oldest and still the key legitimating professional ethic of liberal journalism; it is a guarantee of quality control which asks us to believe that what is being said is valid and believable. The claim of journalistic objectivity is essentially an appeal for trust, even in situations where the facts of a situation may not be fully known.

Today we expect objectivity, or at least the striving for it, to be the normal condition of journalistic work, to the extent that we are hardly aware of its presence. But journalism was not always concerned with objectivity. Early journalists, fighting for liberal democratic rights of free expression and intellectual dissent in authoritarian feudalistic societies, were partisan, placing themselves in the service of the radical bourgeoisie and its struggle for intellectual pluralism; against the feudal establishments of Europe and pre-revolutionary

America, which sought to hold freedom back. They were reporters of news, but also campaigners who wrote revolutionary tracts on the rights of man (the rights of women came later). As late as the early nineteenth century newspapers in both Europe and North America were still 'party organs', infused with ideological commitment and political passion. In the course of that century, however, and into the twentieth, objectivity emerged as the central ethic of the maturing profession of journalism. That it did so, then, and in that form, was the product of three broad trends then apparent in capitalist society: the *philosophical, technological* and *economic.*

The philosophy of objectivity

The nineteenth century was a period of rapid scientific and technical progress (see below) – the age of the industrial revolution, fuelled by the dramatic wealth-creating power of capital and by the intellectual revolution in science which accompanied it and made it possible. In the nineteenth century scientists and philosophers of knowledge began to make sense of the natural world in terms of what became known as 'positivism'. Positivism became the dominant methodology – the dominant *ideology* – of science, because of its success in underpinning and facilitating the achievements of the scientific revolution.

Positivism implied a certain approach to the production of knowledge (the study of knowledge production is known as *epistemology*), based on observation, experimentation and deduction. It assumed that there was such a thing as absolute truth, to be discovered by the empirical work of the observer, that 'reality is accessible by simple observation' (Entman, 1989, p. 50), that there was a real world of absolute certainties to be known and understood and from which scientific laws could be generated. Positivism asserted the existential separation of the observer from the observed. The observer (scientist) could stand apart from the observed and discover 'truth' about it if he or she applied the correct procedures.

As the social science disciplines (history, sociology, economics) developed in the nineteenth century, they too pursued a positivist approach in an effort to acquire the prestige and legitimacy of the natural sciences. And by the mid-1800s so too did the emerging profession of journalism, as creator of 'the first draft of history', and aspiring to status and credibility beyond that of the merely literary:

journalists wanted to believe that they could stand apart from the real world, observe it dispassionately and report back with 'the truth'. In the late nineteenth century, for the first time, 'concern for a definitive historical reality appeared in the journalistic sphere'(Schiller, 1981, p. 86).

Technology

The philosophically inspired search for objective truth was encouraged and accelerated in the nineteenth century by the invention in the late 1830s of photography, a recording medium of unprecedented denotative accuracy and apparent truthfulness, which for the first time 'technologised' the artificial representation of people and events.[1] Photography seemed to justify the philosophical belief in absolute truth by appearing to document reality in an unmediated way (that is, without the subjective intervention of the observer). Of course, photography was from the outset as essentially subjective and creative a representational technique as painting or writing, involving aesthetic choices at the level of framing, lighting, angle and so on. News photography is as subjective as any other kind of photography and can be encoded in a highly value-laden way. But photography *looks* like the real thing to the human eye. It *appears* to be true, and its growing use from the mid-1840s inevitably strengthened the journalistic claim to objectivity. This claim was further enhanced in the twentieth century by the invention of moving pictures and the application of filmic techniques in journalism. To this day, television news is the most 'trusted' of all journalistic products because of the denotative accuracy with which it records events.

Economics

Objectivity was the by-product of a developing commercial market for journalism in the nineteenth century. As historians have noted (for example, see Curran and Seaton, 1997), this process led to the *commodification* of journalism and increased the need of journalistic media to sell their product (news) to ever broader markets. As newspapers became capitalist enterprises in the 1830s and after, they gradually lost their party affiliations and worked to establish their independence as producers of truth. The news agencies which formed in the nineteenth century had a particular need in this respect, since their information had to sell to newspapers of all political affiliations and styles. Newspapers remained committed, of course, lending their 'public voice' to this party or another, but the subjective tone of editorials, commentary columns and other formats where opinions are overtly displayed were usually separated from the paper's *objective* reportage. Even the most proactively partisan titles, such as the pro-Tory British tabloids of the 1980s and early 1990s, maintained at least the appearance of a distinction between 'fact' and 'comment'.

Thus, for philosophical, technical and commercial reasons, objectivity had by the early twentieth century become the principal legitimising ethic, the key 'strategic ritual' underpinning the status of journalism as 'truth'. Henceforth, journalists would routinely invoke the concept of objectivity 'in order to process facts about social reality' (Tuchman, 1972, p. 661). Objectivity became 'a cornerstone of the professional ideology of journalists in liberal democracies' (Lichtenberg, 1991, p. 216).

The rules of objectivity

Despite some criticisms of the concept, which we will discuss shortly, objectivity continues to closely structure the work of journalists in liberal democratic societies and to be cited by them frequently in defence of their output. So what does it involve? Three characteristics of 'objective journalism' can be identified:

- the separation of fact from opinion;
- a balanced account of a debate;
- the validation of journalistic statements by reference to authoritative others.

First, objective journalists are not expected to be devoid of opinions, nor to entirely refrain from expressing them. Indeed, their opinions are often what audiences most want, in the form of editorials, commentary columns and other categories of 'authored' journalism, but the distinction between fact and opinion, information and commentary, news and analysis must, as was noted above, be clearly made in the journalistic text. The organisational structure of news outlets reflects this in designating some journalists as *reporters* of relatively value-free information and others as *commentators* (columnists and leader writers) on that information.

Second, liberal pluralist principles (the normative paradigm) decree that 'the underlying purpose of the media [is] to help discover truth, to assist in the process of solving political and social problems by presenting all manner of evidence and opinion as the basis for decisions' (Siebert, 1956, p. 51). Fulfilling this purpose requires, above all, 'balance' in the representation of competing positions on issues. As Robert Entman puts it:

> Objectivity rules contain two primary requirements. *Depersonalisation* demands that reports refrain from inserting into the news their own ideological or substantive evaluations of officials, ideas or groups. *Balance* aims for neutrality. It requires that reporters present the views of legitimate spokespersons of the conflicting sides in any significant dispute, and provide both sides with roughly equivalent attention. (1989, p. 30)

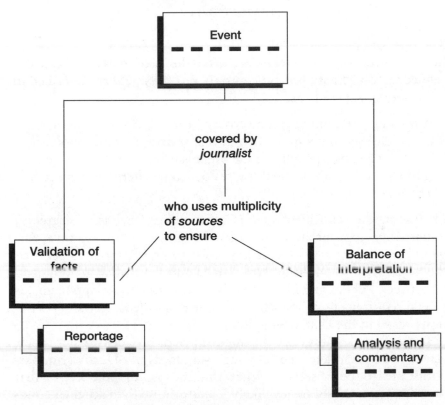

Figure 4.1 Objective journalism

Last, although a journalist strives to convince the audience of the credibility and trustworthiness of her or his statements, these must be founded on facts which can be seen to be independent of the journalist. The journalist has licence to interpret facts but cannot be seen to invent them.

Applying these rules in practice gives us the pyramidical structure of the classic journalistic narrative (Figure 4.1) in which news is sourced, reported and interpreted. In the case of the Monica Lewinsky scandal, for example, *Newsweek* magazine received information about the story before it had become public but decided not to publish on the grounds that her extremely serious and newsworthy allegations could not be validated to its satisfaction. As a result, the story was broken not by a pillar of the objective journalistic establishment, but by the *Drudge Report*, a hitherto obscure and self-confessedly scurrilous and unreliable internet gossip page.

Impartiality

The rules of objectivity apply to both print and broadcast journalism but the latter, since its emergence after the Second World War, has refined the objectivity principle into that of *impartiality*, described in one sociological study as:

> a peculiar conception of objectivity fostered in broadcast news
> . . . an allegation is quoted from one source, a counterpoint is
> made by a spokesperson for the organisation subject to the alle-
> gation, and truth is held to reside somewhere in between.
> (Ericson *et al.*, 1990, p. 39)

In Britain, the refinement of *due impartiality* (that is, a degree of impartiality appropriate to the issue in question; for example, one would not expect a broadcast journalist to be impartial as between the illegal Irish Republican Army (IRA) and the British government, or between Pol Pot and his Cambodian pro-democratic opponents) is a legal requirement of the BBC and other broadcast news organisations based in the United Kingdom.

In the United States, too, the importance of broadcast news is perceived to be such that especially high standards of objectivity/impartiality are to be observed. What this means, in practice, is that broadcast journalists are less likely to editorialise than are their counterparts in the press; they are more likely to attempt to maintain a visible detachment from the events they are reporting, and to refrain from commenting on those events. Broadcast news does include commentary in the form of 'quotes' from accessed pundits and other 'accredited witnesses' to the events being reported, but by convention the presenter or anchor in television or radio news is a neutral figure who can reliably be trusted by all.

In recent years, as the number of broadcast news outlets, and thus competition for each individual organisation, has increased (see Chapter 6), this convention has begun to be relaxed to allow more room for opinion and analysis from key journalists. The commercial value of well-founded, authoritative opinion is enhanced in a more competitive broadcast news market, where viewers and listeners have much more choice of provision than ever before. Thus, within the heightened objectivity of the broadcast news form as a whole, senior journalists find an increased freedom to 'intervene' with commentary and analysis, moving closer to the tradition of the print media.

The critique of objectivity

If objectivity is the mantra chanted by journalists when they wish to signal their privileged status as society's truthtellers, it is also the first target selected by those who wish to criticise or demystify that status. When Lenin was constructing an ideological justification for the Bolshevik approach to journalism, with its stress on partisanship and ideological commitment, he denounced the principle of objectivity as 'bourgeois objectivism' (McNair, 1991). From a materialist perspective he, and Marxist thinkers in general, argued that since all societies were economically, politically and culturally stratified along class lines, the notion that there could be any absolute truth in journalism was false. Bourgeois journalists wrote what was true for the bourgeoisie, but not necessarily for anyone else. Wrapping their work in the packaging of objectivity was, he maintained, an ideological fiction intended to secure broad social acceptance of the dominant bourgeois world-view. There was no neutral, value-free perspective from which the journalist could observe and report. All perspectives reflected the world-view of a class: the only important question was on which side, which class, was the journalist.

This materialist critique, which informed the journalistic practice of the Soviet state after 1917, has underpinned the thinking of Marxist critics of the media in the capitalist world itself. Running through the critical sociology of journalism of the 1960s, 1970s and 1980s, as Chapter 2 indicated, was the assumption that all cultural production, including journalism, is ideologically 'loaded' (biased) in favour of the dominant groups in society and that the concept of objectivity is itself part of the legitimising ideology of capitalism. Objectivity may be a strategic ritual for professional journalists; it is also, for adherents to the dominance paradigm, a strategic legitimising rhetoric for the output of cultural institutions which are owned and/or controlled by a small elite of capitalist entrepreneurs and establishment figures. Objectivity masks the value-laden, selective nature of news and journalism and its deeply pro-systemic bias. Daniel Hallin, for example, argues that

> Freedom from ideological bias is an essential principle of the ethic of the professional journalist. What this means in practice, however, is that journalists are loth to take sides when explicit political controversies develop. Where consensus reigns, they rely as heavily as anyone else on the symbolic tools that make up the dominant ideology of their society. (1986, p. 50)

These arguments were explored in Chapter 2. Here we note that the materialist approach implies a fundamental rejection of the objectivity principle and acceptance of the belief that all truths are relative to the class perspective of the observer.

Cultural relativism

A comparably sceptical approach to the objectivity principle is shown by the proponents of cultural relativism, a post-war trend in Western philosophy which, like materialism, rejects the notion of absolute truth (though not exclusively from a Marxist perspective). Cultural relativists point out, following the scientific discoveries of Einstein and others, that even the physical world changes with the position of the observer (Einstein's theory of relativity; Heisenberg's Uncertainty Principle). How much more 'relative', therefore, is the social world which is journalism's subject? What and who we are structures, to some extent, how and what we see: a man's view of truth is different in some respects from that of a woman; a black woman's from a white man's; an American's from a German's; and so on. There is no single absolute truth but a multiplicity of available accounts from which the journalist has to select and construct 'news'.

The perception that the rules of objectivity are being applied validates that selection and gives it preference over others, but it is a selection nonetheless; at best it is a *relative* rather than an absolute truth.

There are, from this perspective, three categories of the real:

1. the world as *is* (and would be, with or without the presence of human observers);
2. the world as *perceived* by human observers;
3. the world as *reported*.

The cultural relativist approach declares that there is no obvious or automatic correlation between these three levels or dimensions of the real. As sociologists we can say that getting from category 1 to category 3 is a complex social process which changes 'the real' as it goes, in the same way that measuring the temperature of a liquid changes that temperature.

This is not as controversial an idea as it looks. Few journalists would now maintain or believe that they can actually *achieve* objective truth, hoping instead that they can approach the ideal with sufficient rigour to win social acceptance for what they produce as news. This means conforming as closely as possible to the rules listed above and reporting as fairly and accurately as possible within the constraints operating without denying that an alternative reading of events may be available.

'New journalism'

In the 1960s a group of US journalists, frustrated by the fetishisation of the objectivity principle and the limits which (they believed) it placed on their work, broke free of the conventions of their profession and began to develop a subversive, 'anti-objective' style which became known as *new journalism*. The new journalism movement intentionally set out to undermine the notion of objectivity by combining the techniques of journalism with those of literature, and to demonstrate that all supposedly objective accounts of reality are highly subjective. These journalists were not Marxists by any means, although they were strongly influenced by, and part of, the 1960s counter-culture. But they shared the materialist suspicion of and disdain for the idea of a rarified, neutral journalism which could more accurately report the real by removing the subjective opinions of the reporter.

One of the pioneers of the new journalism movement, Tom Wolfe, explained it as part of the desire of US journalists (and many countries had similar movements) to liberate themselves from the constraints of 'hard news' and 'scoop reporting' and move beyond 'the conventional limits of journalism' (1978, p. 35). The result was a style which allowed for, indeed encouraged, the journalist's involvement in the story. Rather than cultivating an aloof, artificial objectivity, journalists got in amongst the action before reporting it back through the prism of their subjective impressions of events. The subjectivity of the human agent in the journalistic process was embraced rather than denied, exploited rather than negated, making new journalism comparable in some respects to fiction writing:

> It was more intense, more detailed, and certainly more time-consuming than anything that newspaper or magazine reporters, including investigative reporters, were accustomed to. They [the new journalists] developed the habit of staying with the people they were writing about for days at a time, weeks in some cases. They had to gather all the material the conventional journalist was after – and then keep it going. It seemed all important to be there when dramatic scenes took place, to get the dialogue, the gestures, the facial expressions, the details of the environment. The idea was to give the full objective description, plus something that readers had always had to go to novels and short stories for: namely, the subjective or emotional life of the characters. (p. 35)

Another key figure in this subversion of the objectivity ethic was Hunter Thompson, author of the novelistic *Fear and Loathing in Las Vegas* (1972) and *Hell's Angels* (1967). Thompson also gained a reputation as an unconventional reporter of presidential campaigns, and a savage critic of Richard Nixon in and out of office. He defined his approach – which he described as 'gonzo journalism' – as:

> a style of reporting based on William Faulkner's idea that the best fiction is far more true than any kind of journalism – and the best journalists have always known this. Which is not to say that fiction is necessarily 'more true' than journalism – or vice versa – but that both 'fiction' and 'journalism' are artificial categories; and that both forms, at their best, are only two different means to the same end. (1980, p. 114)

Thompson's contempt for the strategic rituals of his journalistic colleagues is revealed in the following reflection on, and justification for, his anarchic, subjective style:

> The only thing I ever saw that came close to Objective Journalism was a closed circuit TV setup that watched shoplifters in the General Store at Woody Creek, Colorado. (p. 114)

The new journalists were most associated with print, but ever since their appearance in the 1960s their rejection of the objectivity ethic has been influential in shaping forms of journalism, both print and broadcast, which seek to acknowledge and give free rein to the element of subjectivity in the reportage of human affairs. Some of these experiments, such as those contained in Ryszard Kapuscinski's books about political dictatorship, have indeed produced a journalism which can justifiably be called 'more true' than fiction.[2] Others, like aesthetic experiments through the ages, have failed. What is certain, however, is that the best journalism of the new millenium will be that which acknowledges the limitations of objectivity and finds new ways to bypass those limitations while preserving the believability of journalistic discourse.

Objectivity as structured bias

Although designed to win audience credibility the professional ethic of objectivity can, under normal circumstances, lead to bias in favour of the powerful. The pursuit of objectivity, in other words, does not mean freedom from political or ideological bias. Indeed, that very pursuit can lead to what C. Richard Hofstetter called in 1976 *structural bias*. Referring to television in particular (although the argument would apply equally to the press and radio) Hofstetter stated:

> its source [structural bias] would be the essential nature of television and the organisation of television news, the desire of the people in the business to do their jobs according to the medium's established professional standards, and to be paid well and promoted for doing so. (quoted in Ranney, 1983)

Judith Lichtenberg makes a similar point in relation to the journalist's routine dependence on validating sources, noting how this dependence produces bias in favour of the powerful:

> Among the canons of objective journalism is the idea that the reporter does not make claims based on her own personal

observation, but instead, attributes them to sources. Yet sources must seem credible to perform the required role, and official, government sources – as well as other important decision-makers in the society – come with ready-made credentials for the job. In addition, they often have the skills and the resources to use the news media to their advantage. Yet such sources are not typically disinterested observers motivated only by a love of truth. (1991, p. 227)

The organisational demand for 'source credibility' combines with the time pressures imposed by the news production process to favour establishment sources. The pace of modern journalism requires that 'both the factual accuracy and the significance of news cannot be taken for granted. For [many categories of] stories this is achieved by routine reference to the institutional order for sources of material' (Murphy, 1991, p. 13). Elite groups in all walks of life are the favoured sources of journalists (Chapter 8 examines how this dependence can be exploited by political actors in the design of source strategies). Conversely, journalistic definitions of who is and who is not an important or legitimate validating source, reinforced by the convenience of accessing some sources over others, may lead to the exclusion of voices which have something relevant to say on an issue. And this is not just a matter of professional practice and organisational constraints. Journalists also bring *cultural* assumptions about source credibility to their work. These will reflect, in the main, elite–establishment views. In news stories about interest rates and inflation, for example, the great majority of accessed voices are financial analysts working for commercial companies. Although these are clearly knowledgeable sources they are not, as Lichtenberg puts it, 'disinterested', and may have different perspectives from other groups in society on, say, the optimal levels of inflation and unemployment which a government should seek to maintain. Why, we might ask, should broadcast news routinely access a financial analyst of Kleinwort Benson and not the general secretary of the car workers' union; why the head of the employers' federation and not the representative of the employees? Is one less biased than the other? Clearly not. But one (usually the one with financial, institutional or political status) is routinely assumed to be a more reliable and authoritative source than the other. Entman argues, therefore, that 'objectivity facilitates the manipulation of news slant. With knowledge of objectivity rules and other news norms elites can concentrate their resources where it will most benefit their press coverage' (1989, p. 38). The professional ethic of objectivity guarantees elite access to the news, since it means that 'journalists have to interview legitimate elites on all major sides of a dispute' (p. 37).

The mix of cultural assumptions and professional constraints which tend towards structural bias in journalism is a factor in their work which many journalists are aware of and have sought to address. A senior figure in the BBC's News and Current Affairs Directorate acknowledges that the broadcast journalist must go beyond a rigid adherence to the rules of objectivity, seeking out stories and reporting issues which are neglected by the favoured sources and being 'open' to alternative sources. As he puts it, 'we [the BBC] have a duty to get minority views on air in a variety of idioms'.[3] How this can best be done, while staying within the conventions of television news, is a matter of ongoing debate for broadcast journalists.

News values and journalistic style

Journalism is by necessity (the time and space available for news is not infinite) a selective account of reality. So journalists acquire, as part of their professionalisation – through training, peer group pressure and newsroom discipline – 'instinctive' news sense (Boyd, 1988), a structure of values which can be applied to the multitude of events occurring in the real world, allowing them to be sifted and hierarchically placed. One former editor states that 'no journalist works outside a tightly scripted brief, a set of news values recognised by everyone within a given paper' (Greenslade, 1997b).

These news values define which events, of all those happening at any time in the world, will be selected for coverage. Galtung and Ruge (1973), in their classic essay, identified several key criteria of news value which are still operative, such as proximity – events happening close by are more newsworthy than those happening at a great distance, all other things remaining equal. Some additional contemporary news values which emerge from observation of the main news media include *deviation*: events which can be reported as disruptions or breakdowns of normality (natural disasters); deviations from social or cultural norms of behaviour and morality (particularly sexual; philandering clergy, for example, are always newsworthy, as in general are lapses of morality or ethics by professionals such as doctors, lawyers and, dare one say it, university lecturers); and lifestyle deviance (in the 1970s, looking like a punk rocker was enough to make one newsworthy).

There are, of course, many categories of deviance, some of which are more newsworthy than others – anything involving sex is immensely newsworthy, as is crime, and the combination of the two in a particular event is doubly newsworthy (sex crimes, crimes of passion).

Newsworthiness also accrues to the doings of elites in all walks of life, but especially politics, the entertainment industry and sport (which is really part of the entertainment industry). People defined as important by their position in government, or their fame and fortune, are automatically newsworthy, even if they have done nothing which might reasonably or statistically count as a deviation from the norm. For some members of the elite, mere *celebrity* is enough to guarantee news coverage (one can be famous for being famous); for others, such as those who govern us, elite status comes with a political and moral *authority* which endows his or her actions and statements with enhanced newsworthiness.

The murder of Gianni Versace in July 1997 illustrates how contemporary news values work. Here was a tragic event involving proximity (in the cultural, rather than geographical sense – Versace was a familiar icon of western popular culture); deviation, in two senses: Versace was murdered, and he was gay. Moreover, he was murdered by a 'gay serial killer'/spurned lover; and celebrity – Versace was a fabulous figure in his own right, associated with the likes of Princess Diana and Elton John. In all of these ways Versace's death in Miami – bearing in mind that murders in that city are relatively common and would not normally attract headline coverage, even in the United States where the incident took place – was of exceptional newsworthiness and received correspondingly extensive coverage throughout the world.

By contrast, the sectarian killing of Bernadette Martin in Northern Ireland around the same time was given only minimal reportage outside the province. This story, like Versace's, was about a cruel murder, but it did not involve celebrity. Nor, tragically, was it deemed by news editors to constitute sufficient deviation from the norm in that part of the world. For the British and international media this story was just another example of the murderous Irish behaving to each other as they have always done, and was virtually ignored. Observing the difference between coverage of the Versace and Martin killings one commentator suggested that 'the enormous disparity in [the media's] response to these killings poses profound questions. About news values. About the cult of celebrity. About our culture' (Greenslade, 1997a).

The article from which this quote is extracted was written in July 1997, shortly before the occurrence of one of the biggest news stories of the late twentieth century – the death of Princess Diana in a car crash. Coverage of this event did nothing to diminish the relevance of the 'profound questions' referred to above, nor did it help answer them. The fact and circumstances of Diana's death, and the spectacular life which had preceded her tragic end, conformed to all the criteria of newsworthiness, and then some, as coverage progressed from a story of celebrity downfall to one of national mourning and popular anger towards, first, the paparazzi who pursued her into that Parisian tunnel, and then the Royal in-laws who appeared (and were portrayed by the media as) cold and aloof from the tragedy. The importance of this event in British culture, and its implications for politics and the constitution, were never in dispute, but many observers questioned the way in which the British media elevated it to such unprecedented heights of newsworthiness in the first week of September 1997.

Concern about the significance of prevailing news values is echoed by many professional journalists. Although some system for allocating newsworthiness, some way of sifting reality, is essential for a journalist, 'prevailing news values can sometimes be a distorting mirror on the world' (Boyd, 1988, p. 165), reflecting and endorsing an elitist, fame and wealth obsessed moral structure. If news values can be viewed as an expression of social values, then the news values prevailing in liberal democratic societies refer to a world which is ethnocentric, elite-orientated and focused on 'negative happenings' (good news is no news). British television news presenter Martyn Lewis generated public debate in 1993 with a call for less journalistic emphasis on 'bad news'. Of broadcast news in particular he argued that it routinely overdoes the negative and downplays the positive, leading to, for example, unremittingly gloomy images of Africa and other foreign locations and an exaggerated picture of the incidence of crime and other social problems at home (1993).

Lewis's views were widely reported, before being dismissed by most of his colleagues in the profession as naive. Those who supported his call for more 'good news' were greatly outnumbered by proponents of the counter-argument that there is no such thing as good or bad news in the abstract, just facts, which audiences and journalists may interpret positively or negatively, depending on their viewpoint. This is somewhat misleading, however. Western journalists could, if they chose, adopt news values which placed greater stress on the positive happenings of political, social and economic life. Some already do in a limited way, as in the '. . . and finally' segment of ITN's primetime *News At Ten* bulletin. '. . . And finally' caps this programme's account of the day's events with a humorous, touching or quirky tale intended to balance the stories of drama, confrontation and tragedy which will on most days have made up the rest of the bulletin. It represents a symbolic statement of the idea that, notwithstanding the preponderance of 'bad news', life is not without its positive dimension, and that we, the audience, should put things into perspective, not get depressed, not be overwhelmed by the negativity of the world as seen through the news prism.

To move from this tokenism to a more systematic and sustained emphasis on the positive would require no less than a redefinition of what news is: a shift away from the notion that news is essentially the reportage of problematic reality to an alternative, authoritarian view of news (see Chapter 5) as constructive social engineering, uplifting and inspiring its audience as they face the challenges and setbacks of life. Such an Orwellian approach is unlikely to find favour in the contemporary professional culture of most Western journalists, because it contradicts a long-established view of their work as the reporting 'of what's out there'. Nor is it apparent that audiences would accept the credibility of an artificially 'happy' view of the world from their news.

The grammar of news

News values broadly determine which types of events are important to the journalist and which are not. The news form, however, imposes further constraints on the kinds of stories which can be told and tends to favour narratives of event over process, effect over cause and conflict over consensus. In mainstream television news few stories can claim more than two minutes of coverage, requiring that the complexities and messiness of events be glossed over. If they cannot be, the event may not be reported. The complex histories and processes underlying most events cannot easily be translated into televisual terms. For the same reason, it is easier for broadcast news journalists to prioritise effects over causes, such as in the case of an industrial dispute. The filming and interviewing of inconvenienced airline passengers at an airport is easier, more televisual, than is narrating the progress of 18 months of negotiations which led up to the dispute taking place. And, since news values prioritise deviation from the norm, conflict is favoured over 'absence of conflict', meaning that one explosion of violence in a former war zone may be more newsworthy than the preceding 18 months of peace.

Journalists do not consciously set out to 'distort' reality by their adherence to these news values and formal conventions. Some are imposed on them by the technical limitations of their medium. Print journalists, for example, can go into much more background detail and expository context than can their colleagues on television news, a fact which, given the pre-eminence of the latter as a news source, seriously concerns observers such as Walter Cronkite. For him, 'Those who get most of their news from television probably are not getting enough information to exercise intelligently their voting franchise in a democratic system' (1997). It might be argued, on the other hand, that before television the people who are now dependent on it had very little regular news and that a compressed televisual journalism is considerably better than none at all.

Other features of news value and grammar are acquired in the journalistic training process, whereas others still may appear to be instinctive and common-sensical. The key point to note is that, whatever else they are, they are cultural, conventional and changeable, and in this respect, as in others (see Chapter 6), the market is king. The most dramatic and 'negative' stories, those with the most deviation in the form of sex, crime, scandal or combinations of all three, are also the most popular. People in liberal capitalism like their news to be full of royal divorces and aristocratic adultery, celebrity cocaine sniffing and serial sex crime. Good news may or may not be 'no news', but it is certainly not profitable news, and until, if ever, it becomes so there is no reason to think that existing criteria of newsworthiness are going to change significantly in the medium term.

$\begin{vmatrix} 5 \end{vmatrix}$

The political environment

This chapter focuses on the political determinants of journalism. The form of the political environment defines more than any other set of considerations the functions which the journalist is expected to perform in a given society, acting as a frame within which the parameters of journalistic activity are drawn. Whether functioning in the context of a liberal democratic or an authoritarian political system the journalist is perceived by the politicians, and by those who would influence the politicians, to be a key cultural player, the successful influencing of whom (by whatever means necessary) is worthy of considerable expenditure of resources.

The political environment

To study the relationship between journalism and politics is to assume, as German sociologist Josef Ernst puts it, that 'News is a product of biases which derive from the foreknowledge individual journalists have about their own political environment and the pressures this environment places on their work' (1988, p. 126). As the great Bolshevik Lenin once said, partly in justification of his own political party's intolerance of dissenting journalists, 'to live in society, and be free of it, is impossible'. Journalists, he meant, are not free agents – a statement which applies as much to democratic societies as to non-democratic ones. Nor *could* journalists be entirely free, if one thinks about it, despite the ambitious demands of liberal democratic theory. They, like most other professional groups, must work within a political environment which contains a certain amount of regulation, control and constraint, exercised through a variety of formal and informal channels. Sometimes these controls and constraints are justified by the needs of good government and social cohesion; sometimes they are the product of political self-interest (for a discussion of the political, economic and organisational constraints on media freedom in liberal capitalist societies, see McQuail, 1992).

Journalism, as the 'watchdog' profession, plays an important role in defining where that line is drawn. For this and other reasons related to their privileged place in the culture, journalists must constantly struggle against the political apparatus for their freedom to report and analyse events, and be prepared to defend this role against the state's tendency, and that of the government of the day (the two are not the same in a democracy), to control and restrict the flow of information. This frequently puts them in the front line of political debate and conflict.

The extent to which the political environment shapes the journalist's work, and the extent of the journalist's power to resist that shaping and act autonomously of the political world, is the product of four variables, which will be discussed in the next four sections of this chapter.

The nature of the political system

Most fundamentally, the historically determined, culturally specific form of a society's political system determines the *legal* principles by which information flows within it and the degree of *legislative* freedom enjoyed by its cultural producers. Both elements are key to the work of the journalist.

It is useful to remember at this point that most societies, throughout most of human history, have been *authoritarian* in character, ruled by individuals, families, clans or parties which have monopolised political power for themselves and ruthlessly suppressed dissenting voices. For most of human history, furthermore, the suppression of dissent was carried on in the absence of media, of journalists or of populations capable of reading what journalists, had they existed, might have written. The key ideological influence in such societies was organised religion, which told people what to do and think, backed up by the application of physical force by the state when the people disagreed.

Liberal democracy

The modern journalistic form, as has been noted, emerged out of the struggle of the radical, revolutionary bourgeoisie of early modern Europe, with the outmoded feudal dictatorships holding back their economic and political ascendancy. For this reason it developed alongside the evolution of liberal democratic political systems and came to embody the principles of intellectual freedom and pluralism which we associate with democracy. Consequently, societies such as the United States, France and Britain which have been formed through the rejection (often violent) of authoritarianism are characterised by a corresponding liberalism in respect of journalism.

Liberal democracy implies a low degree of political control of the media and a high degree of tolerance amongst political elites for the unwelcome and critical things which journalists in such a system will write and say. More than that, a liberal democratic political system *demands* journalistic criticism of elites as a condition of its legitimacy.[1] Critical and pluralistic journalism is viewed as a safeguard against the possibility of a return to authoritarian rule and as a watchdog over the abuse of political power by those to whom it is entrusted by the people in elections. Woodward and Bernstein's coverage of the 1972 Watergate break-in and its cover-up exemplifies the freedoms enjoyed by journalists in a liberal democracy such as the United States, and the *Guardian* newspaper's coverage in the mid-1990s of the 'cash for questions' parliamentary scandals (Figure 5.1), provides a more recent British example of what journalistic freedom is supposed to lead to in practice. In both cases the writings of journalists contributed substantially to the removal of tainted governments. In both, journalists and their editors defended their work as the legitimate exercise of their responsibilities in a liberal democracy.

Leftist critics of liberal democratic political systems have, as noted in Chapter 2, been sceptical of the extent to which examples of this kind truly reflect journalistic 'freedom' to attack the 'ruling class', as opposed to being symbolic and superficial attacks on the management of capitalism, which by removing 'rotten apples' from the barrel serve ultimately to strengthen the system and its inherent inequalities. Noam Chomsky and Ed Herman stress throughout their writings on the media the limitations of press freedom in the United States and elsewhere, arguing that it never extends to challenging the real bases of economic and political power. Ralph Miliband (1973) wrote similarly about Britain in the 1970s. Their arguments are valid insofar as journalistic freedom within liberal democratic regimes *is* limited, at

Figure 5.1 'A liar and a cheat'. Source: *The Guardian*

least within commercial and mainstream public media, to criticism of the running of the system rather than the system itself. Radical, even anti-systemic journalism of left and right does exist in pockets, but it has never been a fully viable part of the capitalist media system. But their more mainstream, liberal counterparts have nevertheless enabled important reforms of the system to be made, and by their investigative and expository work contributed much to the 'humanising' of Western capitalism in the twentieth century, widening and deepening its democratic foundations. Journalists in liberal capitalist societies have, as democratic theory insists they should, made economic and political power more accountable rather than less so. With the failure of utopian socialist alternatives to capitalism, the 'watchdog' role of the journalist will become ever more important as a safeguard against the emergence of new forms of despotism in the advanced capitalist societies of the twenty-first century.

Authoritarianism

Authoritarian regimes by contrast, of which there are still many in the world, do not normally allow criticism of their actions by journalists. Such regimes, whether inspired by ideologies of the left or the right, view pluralism and intellectual freedom as subordinate to the interests of the collective (the definition of collective interests typically being monopolised by the regime itself). Criticism of the regime is viewed as treason to class (in the case of Marxist–Leninist inspired governments), Allah (for fundamentalist Islamic regimes) or race (the nazis; the apartheid regime of South Africa). There are in addition what may be regarded as 'gangster' regimes, such as that of Haiti until it was overthrown by US intervention in 1995, which control journalism and other cultural forms for nothing more principled than financial gain.

Authoritarian regimes of whatever kind insist on journalistic deference and conformity to the official line on events, believing – as Lenin put it when he said that 'words were more dangerous than bombs and bullets' – that criticism may lead to political unrest and collapse of the regime. In addition, they often regard journalism as a tool of social engineering, to be put to the service of encouraging social development in a particular direction, and preventing unwelcome trends from taking root. In contrast to the liberal approach, which positions the journalist as a disinterested reporter of events, authoritarian systems enlist journalism unapologetically into the apparatus of ideological control. Soviet journalists, for example, were prohibited from reporting on such problems as crime (with the exception of political crime, or 'dissidence'), economic mismanagement or the spread of HIV/AIDS within the USSR. Instead, they were urged to focus on the positive achievements of Soviet society and to convey by selective reporting of economic and social success stories an image conforming to the utopian predictions of Marxist–Leninist ideology. In their news Soviet citizens learnt not about serial killers, environmental disasters or air crashes (all of which were present in Soviet society) but heroic feats of overproduction in the fishing industry, or the fraternal harmony in which different ethnic groups were alleged to live. Events which contradicted the general picture of successful societal development painted by the Communist Party never achieved the status of news. (For a book-length study of Soviet-era journalism, see McNair, 1991.)

Historians differ as to when the rot of personal dictatorship set in (with Lenin in 1917, or Stalin in the 1920s?), but most agree that what began in the early twentieth century – in the midst of barbaric world war and mass famine – as a sincere and principled critique of 'bourgeois' news values, with their antiproletarian stress on striking workers and revolting peasants, became by the end a means of covering up failure, decay and corruption, to the benefit only of the self-appointed elites in Soviet society.

This distinction between sincerity and cynicism is an important one because, as students of the media in societies which are relatively affluent and conflict-free, we should recognise that there are other societies which, at certain moments in their development, cannot afford the luxury of a free press; which, in times of revolution or war, require a journalism which provides models for emulation and inspiration, rather than dissent and demonstration. There have been and still are societies where, for a time at least, the freedom of the journalist to criticise must be subordinate to the needs of the people to be fed and housed. But the history of the twentieth century shows that, whatever the pressures which have led to authoritarian regimes and which may give them temporary legitimacy, they ultimately, if not subjected to democratic control, decay into corrupt dictatorships. Their journalists, like it or not, gradually become servants of criminal elites.

The international political environment and the national security state

Even democratic societies, in time of genuine crisis (Britain and the United States, for example, during the Second World War) may with good reason apply authoritarian principles to their media for the greater good of the collective, brushing aside the professional ethic of objectivity and turning journalism to the production of propaganda. During the cold war between the capitalist West and the communist East, which lasted for most of the twentieth century and ended only with the collapse of the Soviet state in 1991, most Western journalists were immersed in a political environment characterised by ideological polarisation and the assumption that taking sides was appropriate. Although East and West were not actually at war, and many informed observers disputed the factual basis of the Soviet 'threat', the propagandistic production of 'images of the enemy' became a routine feature of much mainstream journalism (for an account of British television news coverage of the 'new cold war', as Noam Chomsky described it, see McNair, 1988). Chomsky and Herman's powerful analyses of US media coverage of East–West and human rights issues in the years of the cold war convincingly demonstrates its biased, misleading character (see Chomsky and Herman, 1979). Such coverage, and its equivalents in Britain and other countries, was the product of a particular political environment in which virtually the entire globe was divided into friends and enemies and their respective activities glorified or demonised according to their place in the interpretive framework imposed by the cold war.

Since the end of the cold war, and the demise of the Soviet enemy, only Saddam Hussein and Mohammad Gaddaffi have regularly inspired similarly propagandistic coverage. For the most part, however, the international political environment has become much more unstable and volatile, its ideological fault lines less obvious and more blurred. As it has done so, international journalism has lost much of what, in the past, gave it structure and coherence. Wars in the former Yugoslavia, for example, have not been easy for journalists to make sense of, involving as they have done not ideological divisions of left and right, but forms of racism and ethnic prejudice which had been thought to belong to an earlier era.

Political trends

The terms 'liberal democratic' and 'authoritarian' belong at the opposite ends of the spectrum, with most societies falling somewhere in between. Many, such as Taiwan or Korea, are in transition from authoritarian systems to democratic ones, displaying characteristics of both. Journalists in these societies are grappling with the changes in their role which democracy brings, often importing advice and experience from other countries. Others, such as China and Cuba, find it increasingly difficult in a world where communication is ever more accessible and immediate to maintain authoritarian control over media, and one can speculate with some confidence that early in the twenty-first century they will be forced to embrace at least some democratic principles, as the Soviet bloc countries had to in the 1980s and 1990s. Some – a few, fortunately – such as Iran and Afghanistan, have moved towards authoritarianism, where they will remain for as long as their ideologies of Islamic fundamentalism convince or compel their populations to comply. In general, though, it appears that the global political trend is away from authoritarianism and towards democracy, if only because the rapid growth of information and communication technologies such as fax, e-mail and the Internet (see Chapter 8) are having that effect on the exercise of power. For that reason it is not utopian to suggest that the global journalistic community of the twenty-first century can expect to have more freedom and thus more responsibility than did their predecessors in the twentieth.

The political culture

A second factor defining the political environment confronted by journalists is that of *political culture*. This is a less tangible concept than that of 'political system' and is secondary to it, but it is important nonetheless since it describes the informal, non-institutionalised relationships which develop in every society between politicians and journalists over time. For Gabi Wolfsfeld, writing on news coverage of the Middle East conflicts, political culture refers to 'the norms, values, beliefs and practices that define the ways in which each news medium relates to the world of politics' (1997, p. 39) as opposed to the legal frameworks and instruments which are the hallmark of a particular political system.

The distinction made here between political system and political culture means that within, for example, systems defined as 'democratic' there may be great variation in the way journalists approach their work. Even where journalists are formally 'free', as they are in post-Soviet Russia, with laws and a constitional framework guaranteeing their independence from government and the state, they may because of broad cultural and historical traditions be more inclined to partisanship and propagandism than their colleagues in, say, the United States. One of the great challenges faced by Russian journalists in the post-Soviet era has been to 'unlearn' the authoritarian habits and instincts of the system which they (or most of them) gladly left behind in the early 1990s (for an account of the challenges and issues facing journalists in the former Soviet Union, see McNair, 1994). Soviet press theory and editorial practice, based as they were on Marxist–Leninist principles of authoritarian control, rewarded partisanship and commitment over what was officially viewed as the 'bourgeois' concept of objectivity. The journalist was a class warrior, dedicated to the service of the Party and the state.

After 1991, when Russia formally embraced the principles of political and journalistic pluralism, many journalists nevertheless found it difficult to free themselves of the 'genetic memory' (as they themselves called it) of Stalinism. They approached political debates not as objective reporters but as committed voices of one party or another, enthusiastically taking sides. Press and broadcast journalism organisations became identified with particular parties and politicians, to the growing frustration of a newly enfranchised population who wanted not cheerleaders but someone to make sense of an extremely complex and confusing situation on their behalf. Partisanship is, of course, commonplace in the journalism of democratic societies (in the press especially), but with the proviso, as we have seen, that straightforward lies and propagandising are not welcome. In Russia, sacrificing truth to the interests of the favoured politician became for a time the rule rather than the exception. In the presidential election of 1996 even television news organisations abandoned all pretensions to objectivity in their enthusiastic endorsement of Boris Yeltsin and their negative coverage of his Communist opponent, Gennady Zhuganov. Long before that campaign, Russian audiences had grown weary with the unrelenting polemicising of their newspapers and television news bulletins, leading to falling circulations and ratings for Russian journalism.

This partisanship was a *cultural* rather than a *legal* problem for Russian journalists (and similar features have been observed in the post-communist journalism of other emerging democracies, such as Bulgaria and Romania). There were no laws requiring them to beat the drum for Boris Yeltsin or Vladimir Zhirinovsky – on the contrary, journalists volunteered for duty, seeing it as their job to wage ideological warfare rather than report on and analyse with some distancing the competing positions of the newly democratised politics. The politicians, for their part, encouraged journalists to become their allies, and used their considerable powers of patronage to enlist supporters. The problem was thus political *and* professional: indeed, the two factors of journalistic production were intimately linked in the emergence of a political culture not yet free of authoritarian attitudes.

Resolving such a problem – and the excessive partisanship of journalists *was* and still is widely perceived as a problem in Russia – is a matter of changing the 'norms, values, beliefs and practices' listed by Wolfsfeld rather than simply reforming the law. In Russia, therefore, the assistance of many Western journalistic and educational institutions, such as the USAID-funded Internews and the UK-government-funded BBC Marshall Plan of the Mind project, has been welcomed, notwithstanding warnings by some people of the dangers of cultural imperialism. The 'best practice' of journalists in the United States,

Britain, France and other countries has been recognised as a model to be learnt from if the conduct of Russian journalists is to be brought into line with the liberal democratic principles which now underpin the political system, and if journalists are to be equipped to resist the pressures exerted on them by politicians.

All countries have their distinctive political cultures, of course, shaped as Russia's has been by history and tradition. The US tradition leads to a print journalism which is perhaps less partisan than the British. In the United Kingdom, newspapers happily act as cheerleaders for their favoured political parties, often at the expense of 'truth' (although their editors and proprietors would not always admit this). In Britain, also, the political culture of party adversarialism is reflected in a broadcast journalism which is closely regulated and monitored for 'impartiality' (see Chapter 4) – impartiality being defined in relation to broadly equivalent coverage of the competing parliamentary groupings.

In the United States there is a strong political culture of executive accountability, manifest for example in the institution of presidential news conferences. In Britain, by contrast, political journalists who want to report the executive's views (the prime minister's) have to cooperate with a secretive, cliquish system known as 'the lobby' which enforces strict rules of accreditation designed in essence to 'preserve plausible deniability' (for an account of how the lobby system works, see McNair, 1995). In general terms the US culture of 'openness' is acknowledged to contrast sharply with the British tendency to political secrecy, and to have an impact on the reporting practices of journalists in both countries. In the United States freedom of speech is guaranteed by the constitution; in Britain there is no 'bill of rights' which can function as a guarantor of journalistic freedom, rather an accumulation of legislative instruments which often lead journalists into difficulties with political elites. In 1998, however, the Labour government of Tony Blair progressed through parliament its promised Freedom of Information Act, and introduced significant changes to the system of governmental information management. In late 1997 Tony Blair's chief press secretary, Alistair Campbell, announced that henceforth a more direct system of prime ministerial briefing would be permitted, ending the need for journalistic use of the attribution 'sources close to the prime minister'. These and other reforms were intended to encourage a more open political culture and a more open political journalism.

In France, a political culture tolerant of extramarital affairs amongst the elite protected the late François Mitterand from publicity concerning his mistresses and illegitimate child, although their existence was widely known about amongst journalists. In the United States, on the other hand, cultural intolerance of such behaviour brought to an end Gary Hart's 1988 presidential bid. Four years later, Clinton managed to effect a transformation of the political culture so that extensive coverage of Gennifer Flowers's kiss-and-tell allegations did not destroy his credibility as a presidential candidate in 1992. Nor, of course, did the revelations contained in the Monica Lewinsky affair damage his popularity ratings in 1998.

The economic relationship between the journalistic media and the political apparatus

A third political factor of great importance for journalists is their economic relationship to the state: does the political apparatus have any control over their resources which can be employed as a means of exercising pressure? Authoritarian regimes of the left, for example, have tended to monopolise ownership of the media or to wrap media organisations in forms of public ownership which are subject to state financing over which the ruling group has control. In such systems, the state and the government are usually the same thing.

Liberal capitalist countries such as the United States, on the other hand, tend to eschew all public ownership of the media, fearing the political abuses which this might lead to. US journalistic organisations are almost entirely owned by private commercial interests or non-profit-making charities, the only exceptions being the international propaganda producers of the cold war era such as USIA and Radio Liberty/Radio Free Europe, which have in any case changed their role in the post-cold-war world.

The European tradition has fallen somewhere in between these two extremes, with private ownership of the press often existing alongside public ownership of the broadcast media, the latter being pursued in the context of strict limitations on direct political interference by government in media output. In Britain, the exemplar of this public service model, the government of the day sets the level of grant available to the BBC – a sum paid for out of taxation through payment of a fee for possession of a television receiver – but is not permitted to intervene directly in the content of the

BBC's journalism. There is no governmental ownership. In Italy, by contrast, television channels were traditionally viewed as the property (intellectual, if not always economic) of particular parties (Christian Democrat, Socialist and even Communist) and expected to display correspondingly biased journalism.

In general, governments and parties in liberal democracies do not tend to own journalistic media, which would be perceived as propaganda in any case, preferring to exercise control in other, less obvious, ways (see below). One of the main arguments for privatised media in post-Soviet Russia, for example, has been that only this form of ownership guarantees the freedom of the journalist from the politicians (although it does not address the problem of political culture discussed above). In practice, the public–private distinction is not a reliable indicator of how journalists will behave politically, but it does have an obvious bearing on the extent of the politician's *power* over the media.

Elite perceptions of the importance of journalistic media

Finally, we should note that the degree of political pressure likely to be exercised on journalists is closely related to elite perceptions of how important different media are to the formation of public opinion at home and abroad. In Britain the BBC is more frequently attacked by politicians than is the commercial television news provider ITN, not because it is watched and listened to by more people (it is not) but because, as the longest established national news provider, it is perceived to carry the greatest weight as an opinion former and leader. Such perceptions may or may not be true, but their effects on the BBC are no less real for that. Most countries have their 'news media of choice', and it is these which tend to find their output most closely scrutinised by politicians.

Exercising political pressure

The means available to politicians to control journalist media include a mix of formal and informal devices.

Physical force

At one extreme, and most depressingly, violence, including murder, is employed against dissident or troublesome journalists by political elites throughout the world. Violence is used mainly, though not exclusively, by authoritarian regimes and their opponents as a means of preventing unwanted viewpoints from gaining wide currency. In 1997 some 84 journalists were killed as they went about their investigative business worldwide. In Chechnya alone, in 1995–96, 10 Russian journalists were killed in suspicious circumstances.

Sometimes individual journalists are the target; in other cases, the aim is to intimidate the journalistic community as a whole. In many Middle Eastern countries, for example, journalists who have supported or opposed regimes have been assassinated, often on the streets of foreign cities. The apartheid regime in South Africa used violence against its journalistic opponents working from exile in Angola and elsewhere, as did the 1980s death squad regimes of central and south America. More recently, in Algeria a murderous civil war has resulted in many journalistic casualties as fundamentalist militants signal their intolerance of more liberal perspectives. In Russia, where the worlds of politics and organised crime are closely intermeshed, journalists campaigning against corruption have been the victims of kidnapping, beatings and murder.[2] *Moskovsky Komsomolets* correspondent Dimitri Kholodov, for example, was murdered by a conspiracy of army officers in 1994 after he threatened to expose corruption amongst the military.

The law

Though the threat of violence is all too common for journalists in all too many countries, it is fortunately not typical of the politician–journalist relationship in liberal democracies. In the latter, legal means of control are favoured, reflecting in their specifics the political system and culture of the country concerned and the balance of political forces over time as expressed in elections. These then confront the individual journalist as a set of constraints and, when necessary, protections against the abuse of power. Consequently, 'the news is a social and historical form which has been moulded by . . . political interests as expressed in legislation' (Bruhn-Jensen 1986, p. 49), and also by a society's historically evolving views on how best to maintain the political independence of journalism as a 'fourth estate'.

In Britain, for example, broadcast news coverage of election campaigns is governed not just by the broad requirement of due impartiality (see Chapter 4) but also by legislation contained in the Representation of the People Act. This legislation attempts to secure balanced reportage of the main participants in an election contest, in the most important media, at the most crucial time in the political cycle, for the benefit of the populace as a whole. In so doing it acts as a constraint on journalists, who cannot report the views or activities of one candidate in a particular constituency without also reporting the views and activities of his or her opponents. The result is a style of election journalism in the United Kingdom which is often criticised for being too 'tit-for-tat' in its structure. The demand for strict balance, as measured in quantitative 'stopwatch' terms, distorts news values and produces, it is alleged, bored and disinterested viewers.

In general, we can say that journalists in democratic societies work within laws which seek to define and limit their rights and responsibilities and to strike an appropriate balance between the two, sometimes conflicting, categories. In Britain, for example, relatively strict laws inhibit coverage of official information unless authorised by government, while coverage of individual celebrities' private lives is relatively free from restriction, as long as certain other laws (of theft or trespass, for example) are not broken in the process of gathering information. In Britain, too, laws of libel prevent news media from publicising defamatory information about individuals. The late Robert Maxwell frequently used these laws to prevent investigative journalists exposing his corrupt business affairs. As a result, many thousands of people lost their jobs and their pensions (for further detail on British media law, see Welsh and Greenwood, 1997).

In the United States, on the other hand, a prevailing political culture of openness and accountability is reflected in rather less official secrecy legislation and a generally less legalistic media environment than is present in most European countries.

The tensions and contradictions of media law vary in different countries, as do agendas in debates about legal matters. In Britain for most of the late 1980s and early 1990s politicians and opinion leaders (such as journalistic columnists) argued that tighter privacy laws were required to protect members of the royal family and others from intrusive reportage of their personal lives, views which became more vociferous after Diana's death in August 1997. The lack of legislation

preventing 'chequebook journalism' came under attack after the wife
of the serial killer Peter Sutcliffe (the Yorkshire Ripper) was paid for
her story by the *Daily Mail* newspaper. By the mid-1990s, however,
in the wake of Robert Maxwell's exposure as a fraudster, journalistic
coverage of political corruption (the 'sleaze' scandals) and the efforts
of the press to self-regulate their activities through the application of
a meaningful code of practice, the pressure for legal reform had sub-
sided, as people became aware that the powerful stood to gain more
than the public by any tightening of privacy legislation. On the other
hand, and not withstanding the election of a Labour government committed to information openness and transparency, British journalists
continue to fight for greater freedom of official information, more akin
to the system enjoyed by US journalists.

Censorship

Throughout the world, under liberal and authoritarian regimes alike,
journalists are continually required to fight against political censorship. Some censorship is clearly justified (on national security grounds
and in time of war, for example, journalists accept that there should
be constraints placed on what they can report). Some is not. Conflict
arises when journalistic and public organisations disagree with government or the state on which of these categories a particular act of
censorship falls into. The ban on the broadcasting of statements by
members of Sinn Fein in Northern Ireland, for example, imposed by
the Conservative government between 1988 and 1994 was not
directly a matter of national security, having no military value in the
fight against the IRA. Rather, it was acknowledged to be an act of
moral–political censorship of views which the government found
offensive. Journalists whose work was affected by the ban argued
that, irrespective of the offensiveness of Sinn Fein's on-air apologias
for terrorist murders, it was an unjustified and counterproductive act
of censorship which would make martyrs of Sinn Fein and harm the
government's international and domestic image – which it did, until
political developments allowed it to be removed in 1994. After that
in the period up to the 1998 peace agreement, as British television
viewers frequently had occasion to note, the spectacle of a Sinn Fein
representative trying to explain why yet another life had to be taken
by a bomb or a bullet arguably did more harm to the Republican
cause than any ban on their media appearances ever could.

Journalists have been subjected to military censorship in a succession of recent conflicts around the world. In the Reagan administration's invasion of Grenada, for example, or the Bush administration's invasion of Panama, the US news media were shepherded around the margins of the fighting and obliged to construct sanitised, gung-ho pictures of the events, minimising casualties and demonising the enemy to the greatest possible extent. In the Gulf War, too, censorship of the international media corps was a central element of the allies' war-fighting repertoire.

Although usually justified on military grounds – and the lives of combatants, as well as civilians, are a wholly legitimate qualification on a generalised media freedom – the aforementioned examples also had clear political implications. In Grenada and Panama, US governments sought to emerge unambiguously as the 'good guys' against foreign thugs. In the Gulf in 1991, the United States, Britain and their allies required domestic and international public opinion to fall in behind the war effort, and carefully controlled media images of the conflict contributed substantially to achieving that political objective. Old-fashioned censorship of this kind, which dates back at least as far as the Boer War of the late nineteenth century (often described as the first 'media war'), is increasingly used in conjunction with military public relations techniques (see Chapter 8) to encourage a compliant, cooperative war journalism.

On the domestic front, censorship is usually more difficult for a democratically-constituted government to justify. Apart from official secrets legislation and laws of defamation (the form and severity of which vary internationally) there are few generally accepted grounds on which journalists may be required not to report something which would otherwise be newsworthy. This does not stop governments trying to suppress sensitive information, of course – celebrated US examples include Watergate and Irangate, and in Britain the Westland and arms-to-Iraq affairs severely embarrassed the governments of Margaret Thatcher and John Major, respectively – but such efforts do not amount to censorship so much as cover-up, the exposure of which itself often becomes a major news story, capable of damaging or even bringing down a government.

Informal lobbying

Politicians in a democracy may not have the legal means of controlling the media enjoyed by their authoritarian counterparts, but they are no less interested in what the journalists have to say about them. Thus, they have developed a battery of informal lobbying techniques intended to win journalists over rather than coerce them into slavish obedience. Chapter 8 examines political news management techniques related to the content of journalism (such as 'spin doctoring' and 'rapid rebuttal') in greater detail: here we are concerned with the pressures politicians apply to the media as institutions, cultivating their support and discouraging their hostility.

Famous examples of such informal lobbying include Spiro Agnew's 1960s attack – mounted on behalf of the Nixon administration – on the 'liberal' Washington media, just a few years before the Watergate scandal engulfed the president. Political executives frequently let their views on the media be publicly known, particularly if they are critical, in the hope that the weight of their authority may have an impact on the content of troublesome journalists and their managements.

British politician–media relations in the 1970s and 1980s featured Margaret Thatcher's assiduous and highly effective courting of tabloid newspaper editors, as a result of which she won their support throughout her premiership. In return, her government rewarded supportive editors and proprietors with knighthoods and other honours, while Rupert Murdoch was allowed major concessions on media cross-ownership. Thatcher's 'seduction' of the British press contributed substantially to her 11-year dominance of the British political scene.

In turn, Tony Blair's cultivation of the traditionally pro-Tory press after his election as Labour leader in 1994, executed by his press secretary Alistair Campbell, produced an unprecedentedly pro-Labour press in the 1997 general election. Murdoch's support for Labour, like his earlier support for the Conservatives, did not come without a price tag attached, however, and Labour's adoption after 1994 of a markedly more liberal regime of media ownership regulation was clearly a gesture to News International, which stood to gain most from such a policy.

These are examples of positive political pressure (public relations of a sort) in which persuasion, backed up by rewards, is used to secure favourable media coverage. More common, historically, has been negative pressure of the type exerted by Agnew on the US press, or by successive British governments on the BBC. We noted above that the degree of political pressure exerted on journalists is related to the politicians' perception of their importance as news providers and opinion formers. In Britain, the BBC has been pre-eminent as the 'national broadcaster' since its foundation in 1926, and is thus the regular target of political intimidation.

The tendency of governments to put pressure on BBC journalists goes back to the General Strike of 1926, but became more regular after its journalists began to rid themselves of the culture of political deference in the 1950s. Until then, broadcast political journalism had been something of a contradiction in terms, often comprising little more than opportunities for politicians to field a few pre-planned questions from an obsequious and deferential interviewer who would not have dared to upset the guest. This changed with the coming of commercial television in Britain in 1955 (see Chapter 6) and the development of a more investigative, critical, interrogatory journalistic style in an effort to make broadcast news more interesting and viewer-friendly. At the same time, international events generated serious political controversy in Britain, shattering the post-war, late empire consensus which had prevailed since 1945. The Suez Canal crisis of 1956 was the first international event, therefore, in which the British government did not find a compliant media prepared to parrot its line, but a journalism which set out to report the national debate with true objectivity. Former director general of the BBC, Alisdair Milne, has written that 'The Conservatives' disenchantment with the BBC can fairly be dated to Suez and the critical, sometimes jeering, tone of programmes like *That Was The Week That Was*' (p. 58).[3] But it was not only the Conservatives who exerted pressure on the BBC:

> Labour's shock, on coming to power [in 1964], and finding the BBC allowing criticism of them as sharp as anything that had been directed at the Tories, was profound. *Yesterday's Men* [a documentary produced in 1971] compounded that feeling and was a major step along the road to today's perception by the politicians of 'the media' as a hostile political force rather than a necessary channel for dissemination of news and participation in political debate. (Milne, 1988, p. 58)

The continuing pressure which has resulted from this perception was shown in the BBC's handling of the *Real Lives* affair, when a documentary programme profiling leaders of both the Republican and the Unionist movements in Northern Ireland was taken off by the BBC's board of governors after governmental objections. In 1992 the *Panorama* current affairs strand cancelled a programme about the problems of the British economy (inevitably critical of the government), prompting speculation that it was afraid of upsetting the Tories (the official explanation, that the programme was poor quality, was generally regarded as unconvincing).

In October 1995, as the verdict of the O.J. Simpson trial was about to be anounced in Los Angeles, new Labour leader Tony Blair had just delivered a keynote speech to the party's annual conference, with high hopes of its receiving headline coverage on that evening's television news bulletins. To convince BBC news editors that a Labour leader's conference speech was more newsworthy than a celebrity murder in the United States Blair's office faxed them a memo, setting out their case. The BBC resisted Labour's pressure, and led with O.J.'s acquittal. The memo was then leaked to the press and became a story in itself, thereby shedding useful light on the processes by which political elites seek to influence journalism.

In general, political pressures of this kind are greatest around the time of general elections, with all major parties lobbying fiercely to ensure that the BBC gives them a 'fair and impartial' (that is, favourable) coverage. On the eve of the 1997 election the Major government explicitly threatened the BBC with privatisation after the next election (assuming that the Tories had won) if its coverage did not become less 'pro-Labour', as the Conservatives perceived it. Since Labour became the government in May 1997 it has bombarded the BBC with a succession of threats and criticisms, at least as intimidatory as anything initiated by the Conservatives during their 18 years in office.

All parties in Britain play these games, then, although the party in government (or likely to be in government in the future) can threaten with more conviction, since it controls the rate at which the television license fee is set and the broader environment in which threats of privatisation can become real. Governments can also use their powers of regulation to intimidate or 'persuade' privately-owned media organisations to cooperate. The support extended by the News International titles to Tony Blair's Labour Party in the 1997 election was not unrelated, some commentators suggested, to Rupert Murdoch's need for a favourable (or at least, not hostile) climate in the sphere of cross-ownership for the next stage of the expansion of his media empire into digitalisation.

6

The economic environment

The spheres of politics and economics are frequently so interconnected within capitalism as to be difficult to distinguish. We will do so nevertheless, for the reason explained in the introduction, and in this chapter move the focus from the activities of political elites to those elements of the economic environment which shape the journalist's work.

Economic forces impact on journalism in two ways. First, the production of journalism is largely the business of an industry, owned and controlled by private individuals and conglomerates (with notable exceptions such as the BBC in the United Kingdom). Journalism is, in a real sense, the private property of these individuals and conglomerates, and they are free within the law to dispose of and use it as they like. Journalists are employees, strongly influenced by those who own or control their organisations. They are subject to direct economic power in the same way as other employees of capitalist enterprises, although some journalists – the 'star' correspondents and columnists, such as Julie Burchill and Hugo Young in the United Kingdom, and Hunter Thompson and William Safire in the United States – bring their own reputations to the market and use them to 'buy' editorial autonomy.

Second, while journalism is an industry it is also a commodity, offered for sale in an ever more crowded information marketplace. As such, and like all commodities, it must have a *use value* and an *exchange value* for potential customers. It must be both functional and desirable – a fact which has had considerable impact on the content, style and presentation of journalism in recent decades. Journalisms must compete with each other for market share.

In both of the contexts listed here the impact of economics on journalism has generated public concern and debate. On the question of ownership, liberals and critical theorists have consistently warned against the dangers of excessive concentration, whereby media 'barons' come to own more of a particular media sector than might be regarded as healthy for a democratic society. Left-wing critics have been especially vocal in this regard, since the majority of media barons tend to have right-of-centre political views and to put their media interests to the service of conservative ideological causes. But the perceived threat of excessive concentration of ownership is a wider concern. Ted Turner, the founder of CNN, who has watched the Murdoch journalistic empire expand in the United States, is reported to believe that his rival uses 'the media outlets over which he has control to further his political agenda' (Usborne, 1996).

In relation to the workings of the market, many critical observers have argued that the quality of both print and broadcast journalism has been damaged by the need of media organisations to compete effectively on commercial criteria and that the normative role of the journalist in a democratic society has been sacrificed to the business needs of the organisation which employs her or him (Bourdieu, 1998).

This chapter will explore both of these issues, beginning with a discussion of contemporary concerns around the ownership and control of journalistic media, before moving on to the impact of commercialisation on content.

Ownership and control

The structure of ownership and control of journalistic media is important to the sociologist for the obvious reason that 'the person who pays the piper calls the tune'. Economic power translates directly, through media ownership, into cultural power. As Chapter 3 showed, the precise extent and nature of this power, as expressed in media effects, is difficult to assess and measure. Very few analysts, politicians or media entrepreneurs would dispute that it exists, however, and that the sociological implications are significant. The British general election of 1997 was accompanied by another episode in the ongoing debate about the impact of newspaper coverage on citizens' voting behaviour. Did the press on that occasion *affect* the electorate's decision to back the Labour Party for the first time in 18 years, or did it merely *reflect* shifts in public opinion which had taken place long before the campaign started? If the latter, what role did the newspapers play in facilitating those shifts? No one can answer these questions conclusively, but the strong assumption that journalism *has* effects of various kinds has always made media ownership an attractive proposition to entrepreneurs with political ambitions.

The fact that most journalistic media are constituted as large and (since Rupert Murdoch smashed the British print unions and introduced new technologies into the newspaper industry) lucrative capitalist enterprises means that they tend to be pro-systemic in their output. The men (and it is, almost exclusively, men, although Rupert Murdoch's daughter, Elisabeth, could break the mould) who own and control them are key players in the domestic and international capitalist economies within which their media operate. Understandably, they use their media to support those economies, and to preserve socio-political systems which allow them to go on generating profits. They are part of the supporting ideological apparatus of capitalism, using their media to reproduce and reinforce the values of free enterprise, profit and the market. The cultural power of the media, such as it is, is harnessed to the maintenance of certain ideological and political conditions, from which the economic health of the media enterprise derives. Culture, ideology, politics and economics are linked in the output of media organisations in a way that is true for no other sector of capitalistic enterprise.

Within the media as a whole journalists are particularly important in this respect, as Chapter 1 suggested, since their output is often distinguished from the ideological and the value-laden, claiming the status of (more or less) objective truth, disinterested fact, fair and balanced reportage of the world. Harnessing the cultural power of journalism can, in the context of universally accessible mass media, be presumed to have direct economic benefits.

That the journalistic media are used in this way should not be surprising if we assume that their owners are rational economic actors. And yet, throughout the short history of journalism studies, analysts have debated the issue as if it were in some dispute.

Media owners, adherents of the competitive paradigm have argued, typically take a hands-off editorial approach to their properties, leaving their day-to-day management to professional journalists who make decisions about content on professional criteria. This view, if sincerely held, is naive. William Shawcross's biography of Rupert Murdoch shows beyond any doubt (and Murdoch does not bother to waste his valuable time denying it) that he is a leading member of the secretive cross-national elite of top business and political leaders who have sought ever since the Second World War to make the world safe (as they would see it) for democracy (1992). In Australia in the 1970s his newspapers played a key role in the controversial ousting of left-wing Prime Minister Gough Whitlam. In the 1980s, expanding onto the global stage, he positioned himself as an active supporter of Ronald Reagan's aggressive free-market capitalism (and US cultural values in general), using his growing transnational media empire to actively promote it. In Britain, as noted in the previous chapter, Murdoch was even more supportive of Margaret Thatcher's government than he had been of Reagan's and was amply rewarded for it. His newspapers became during her premiership the effective party organs of the Conservative Party, toeing an ideological line just as persistently, and with as much regard for the truth of a story, as did *Pravda* in the old USSR. His newspapers during these years pursued a blatant pro-business, anti-Labour, anti-union bias, on top of the routine sexism, homophobia and xenophobia which made the Thatcher-era *Sun* a byword for the degeneration of journalistic morality and ethics. His employees, policed by their editors, were required to submit copy which reflected the proprietor's ideological and political values. His editors were used to being woken in the early hours of the morning with 'advice' from the proprietor which they were in no position to ignore. Although successful News International editors such as Andrew Neil and Kelvin Mackenzie were given managerial autonomy over the titles for which they had responsibility, they were never more than employees, to be removed when they had become expendable.

Of the need for journalists in general (and not just those who work for News Corporation) to reflect the biases of their proprietors, one practitioner points out that 'to survive and rise in, or on, "the game", you pander to the political prejudices of your paymasters, giving them the stories that you know will make them salivate' (Bevins, quoted in McKie, 1995, p. 128).

While most newspaper proprietors have tended to be politically Conservative the late Robert Maxwell wished to be thought of as being on the left, and used his papers – though with equal disregard for the ethic of journalistic objectivity – to support the British Labour Party, and as what he himself called a 'megaphone' for influencing the political debate in the countries where he owned media. Maxwell, caricatured by the satirical magazine *Private Eye* as a 'life long socialist', was a rare example of a left-of-centre media baron who used the cultural power of his newspapers to pursue a broadly social democratic agenda in Britain, while maintaining good (and for him, profitable) relations with the Communist leaders of the Soviet bloc countries. Notwithstanding his eventual emergence as a corrupt, dishonest bully, he was one of the few exceptions to the overwhelmingly right-wing political character of international media barons in the 1970s and 1980s.[1]

The historical paucity of left-wing media barons has been a major factor in driving the debate about ownership and control. All commercial journalistic organisations are pro-systemic and thus pro-capitalistic. It would be odd if they were not, given that a healthy capitalist economy is in their proprietors' interests as business people. But, many argue, did they need to be so *pro-Conservative* as, in Britain at least, they have been? The British labour movement, by common consent, has been consistently marginalised, denigrated and abused by the British press throughout the twentieth century, despite its social conservatism, democratic credentials and enduring popular support. Despite the wishes of the electorate expressed in many general elections over the years (45% consistently, with the exception of the 1983 election), the British Labour Party had never, until the election of 1997, received anything like a corresponding share of press support. On the contrary, it had suffered a 'press deficit' as the big press proprietors lent the services of their newspapers to the Tories year after year, in election after election. This situation, many believed, was a serious violation of press responsibility in a democracy, and one which needed remedying by various combinations of state subsidy, tax breaks and other governmental supports for a left-wing press.

Liberal perspectives on press ownership – which have always opposed state intervention in the newspaper market on the grounds that it would lead to political censorship (see Chapter 5) – had traditionally sought to minimise the importance of economic ownership by stressing the diversity of editorial stance which a 'free market' generated. The media barons themselves also used this argument. In Murdoch's *Sunday Times* columnist Jonathan Miller pointed out some time ago that

> Walking into a [British] newsagent, readers face a choice of twenty-one national daily and Sunday newspapers owned by ten different groups, eighty-nine regional and local daily papers, 1,500 weeklies and 7,600 magazines and periodicals. The titles reflect every conceivable point of view. (1992)

This is disingenuous, since it ignores the fact that for most of twentieth-century British political history, and despite the formal freedoms enjoyed by the press, editorial diversity has meant in practice overwhelming support for the Conservative Party. The pattern of pro-Tory press bias peaked in the 1987 and 1992 general elections, both of which Labour lost.

But then, in 1992 as the British Conservatives settled into their historic fourth term and the memory of Margaret Thatcher began to fade, something unexpected happened to the British press. After 1993 in Britain, press loyalty to the Conservative Party fragmented, for a variety of political and economic reasons, including the breakdown of the personal relationship many editors and proprietors had with Margaret Thatcher following her resignation, continuing anger with the new Tory leadership at the manner of her departure, a loss of faith in the radicalism of the Major-led Tories, disgust at the air of sleaze, sex and corruption which came to surround the Tories in their final years (and which the pro-Tory press had themselves done much to create) and enthusiasm, shared by the British public as a whole, for the 'radical centre' position adopted by Tony Blair's New Labour party after his election as leader in 1994.

Table 6.1 shows how the British press 'voted' in the 1997 general election by comparison with their stated preference in 1992. Most surprising is the position of Murdoch's News International titles, of which only one behaved in the traditional manner by urging its readers to support the doomed John Major, 'warts and all'. The News International tabloids – the *Sun* and the *News of the World* – completed the slow drift towards New Labour which had been going on since 1994 by coming out firmly for Tony Blair and the desirability of a Labour government. In doing so, it now seems clear, these newspapers were following a leftward shift in the views of their readerships. Moreover, it is reasonable to suppose that, calculating that Labour would be the next government of Britain, Murdoch gambled that support for them before rather than after the election would maximise his prospects of experiencing a sympathetic business environment into the next Labour-led century. Time will tell if he was correct in this calculation, but we can legitimately conclude that, as in Bob Hawke's Australia, Murdoch changed horses for essentially commercial, pragmatic reasons associated with the long-term growth of his business empire. The partial demise of the 'Tory press' in Britain, at least for the time being, signals Rupert Murdoch's endorsement of the new management team at British capitalism plc and merely confirms his power as a proprietor, now being applied to the benefit of the Labour Party rather than its disadvantage.

Table 6.1 Press support for the major political parties in the 1997 general election. Source: Audit Bureau of Circulation

	Conservative	Labour	Liberal Democrat	None	Circulation[a]
Daily papers:					
Sun		✓			3 819 908
Mirror[b]		✓			3 052 362
Star		✓			740 568
Mail	✓				2 153 868
Express	✓				1 220 439
Telegraph	✓				1 132 789
The Times				✓	756 535
Guardian		✓			429 101
The Independent		✓			263 707
Financial Times		✓			319 400
Sunday papers:					
News of the World		✓			4 429 387
Sunday Mirror		✓			2 211 527
People		✓			1 908 363
Mail on Sunday					2 129 376
Sunday Express	✓				1 153 873
Sunday Times	✓				1 331 656
Sunday Telegraph	✓				910 803
Observer		✓			480 426
Independent on Sunday		✓			278 465

[a] Average figures for May 1997. [b] Incorporates figures for *Daily Record* in Scotland.

Exercising proprietorial control

Proprietorial control of journalistic output is exercised, as in any other capitalistic organisation, through the appointment of like-minded personnel in key management positions who are delegated to carry out the boss's will. Journalists who disagree with editorial policy often have their copy 'spiked', or are removed from their positions. This is not to deny that newspaper editors are important figures in their own right, stamping their journalistic and management styles on their titles. When an editor is notably successful in improving a newspaper's market position, or gains a positive reputation for quality, he or she may acquire a relatively high degree of autonomy from the proprietor. Both Kelvin MacKenzie, during his time as editor of the *Sun*, and Andrew Neil on the *Sunday Times* enjoyed this status in their dealings with Rupert Murdoch. But even they – editors of two of the most commercially successful and politically influential British newspapers of the 1980s and 1990s – were liable to receive frequent personal calls from their proprietor and both were eventually promoted out of their editorial seats when Murdoch judged that the time for a change in direction was right.

In some cases, newspapers get guarantees of editorial independence from a prospective buyer, but these are rarely honoured after the transfer is made. Murdoch gave such guarantees in relation to *The Times* and *Sunday Times* because he had to in order to gain control of them, but he replaced key editorial staff as soon as he could or made life difficult for those whom he wished would leave. Someone who is investing millions in a newspaper is going to run it as he or she likes.

The economic fact of life which is proprietorial influence clearly has important sociological implications for the role of journalism. When ownership becomes excessively concentrated in a few hands, the influence of those few on political life increases proportionately (all other things being equal). The liberal critique of journalism (and the materialist–Marxist critique) has therefore always highlighted the evidence of concentration of ownership and campaigned against it (for effective antimonopoly laws, for example). Ironically, perhaps, some aggressively pro-capitalist countries such as the United States have very strict laws in this respect, whereas others, including Britain, operate more liberal regimes.

Evaluating the societal impact of the structure of media ownership is not straightforward. A fairly small number of owners dominate the newspaper market in Britain, but the situation is relatively worse in many other countries. There are those, such as Jonathan Miller in the quote reproduced above, who argue that there *is* sufficient diversity and pluralism in Britain, ranging from the *Guardian* on the left to the *Daily Telegraph* on the right; that there are also successful periodicals of the left and the right (the *New Statesman* and the *Spectator*, respectively); and that it is hardly surprising if the spectrum of mainstream editorial diversity stops short of political extremes. There is, it is argued, no mass market in Britain for an 'authentic' left-of-centre tabloid, as the disastrous experience of the *News On Sunday* proved.[2] What *is* 'the left' anymore, it might be argued, outside the meeting rooms of elitist, doctrinaire factions? There is certainly no mass left on whom a left-of-centre press (that is, more traditionally left-of-centre than the *Guardian*) would depend. The 'legitimate' left – the Labour Party, the trade unions – are, for the moment at least, well served by broadsheets, tabloids and periodicals. State intervention in the market to subsidise politically correct media would be both dangerous, from the democratic perspective, and futile from the commercial.

These arguments are compelling, as Britain enters a prolonged period of Labour government, and the left is apparently on the ascendancy. Unless and until a British Berlusconi comes along who can influence the political environment, as *Forza Italia* did, through control of the media, the pressures for restrictions on media ownership and control are unlikely to be a major priority in the United Kingdom.

Of course, as we saw in Chapter 5 in the discussion of politics, such legislation may still be used, or its use threatened, as a political weapon in the hands of parties competing for media support. Following Tony Blair's election as Labour leader in 1994, and the beginning of the Party's 'courting' of News International, its policy on cross-media ownership became noticeably more liberal, even by comparison with the avowedly free-market Conservatives. Although it is generally acknowledged that ownership rules have to change as the media industries increasingly converge and 'globalise' and economies of scale become available many observers concluded that Labour's new liberalism on the issue was a carrot dangled before News International in order to secure a more sympathetic coverage of its policies. If this was the case, the strategy certainly worked.

The market

Given what we have said thus far about the cultural power of media proprietors it is fortunate that, even where there is identifiably excessive concentration of ownership in a particular media sector, the workings of the information marketplace may militate against the straightforward translation of proprietorial influence into editorial bias. There are a number of market-led constraints on the output of journalistic media, not least of which is the fact that journalism is a commodity and must find a buyer in a competitive environment. This requirement has two implications:

- first, the journalistic text has to acquire an exchange-value (price) from which income and profit largely derive;

- second, where advertising is sought, an audience of a certain *quantity* and *quality* has to be delivered to the advertiser in order to secure the maximum price for space.

The need to find an audience, and an audience of the appropriate 'quality', can overrule the ideological predilections of proprietors, and place limits on their ability to use their media as an instrument of propaganda. When Rupert Murdoch set up Sky News, for example, he did so to gain some respect as a broadcaster, in a market (British television) which placed high value on the quality of broadcast journalism and which he dearly wanted to enter. A loss-making 24-hour news channel, operating under the same guidelines of balance and impartiality as the BBC and ITN, was the price Rupert Murdoch decided to pay for respectability in the United Kingdom media marketplace. So Sky News, since its inception, has enjoyed a much higher degree of editorial independence than have the News International papers and has, as a consequence, been widely praised for the journalistic quality of its content.

Similarly, Murdoch (even before News International's turn to Labour) let the *Sunday Times* contain a wide range of journalistic viewpoints (right, left and downright off-the-wall) because he knew that his youngish, affluent, educated readership would not respond to being patronised and lectured from the right alone.

In these cases the market has shaped content, because the proprietor's business interests come first (even before ideological commitments). When the *Sun* supported Labour in the 1997 election it was in part because this is what Murdoch and his editorial staff believed its readers wanted. Support for New Labour, as already noted, was a rational business decision, of relatively low risk given Tony Blair's abandonment of 'old Labour' ideology, and entirely consistent with News Corporation's global strategy.

Broadcasting

The applicability of what has been said about the press above to privately-owned broadcasting organisations varies from country to country. In the United States, where broadcasting was from its inception regarded as a business, individuals and corporations (increasingly the latter, since no individual in the US market can withstand the financial power of the multinationals for long) have played an important role in shaping the editorial policies and stylistic conventions of news. Ted Turner's Cable Network News illustrates the power of one man to influence the journalism industry, even if he had in the end to cede ownership of his company to the larger Time-Warner corporation.

But private ownership of broadcast news in the United States has not had the perceived negative effects seen in, for example, Italy, where one man (Silvio Berlusconi) succeeded in becoming prime minister at the head of an entirely media-created political party, *Forza Italia*. US broadcast news has no legal obligations to impartiality and balance but the demands of the marketplace, and the premium placed by audiences on the objectivity of news, have acted as an incentive for both the established networks (CBS, NBC, ABC) and new entrants (CNN, Fox) to maintain the highest possible standards of fairness and accuracy in regard to their coverage of public affairs.

As we saw in Chapter 2 critics like Chomsky and Herman insist on the deep structural biases of US broadcast (and print) news organisations, pointing to their function as the propaganda wing of what they call the *National Security State*. Ideological bias *is* certainly a feature of US broadcast news (as it is of all news, everywhere) and can often be best explained in relation to the connections of class and culture which bond media elites with other elite groups in US society. Nevertheless, it has never been the case that the capitalistic form of US television news leads to a narrow partisanship in favour of one party, candidate or public lobby. The biases, to the extent that they exist, are more fundamentally pro-systemic than that.

In Britain, too, commercial broadcast news has to make a profit, like newspapers, but unlike the press must avoid overt political bias in its coverage. In Britain, where the public service broadcaster sets the industry standard in news, the commercial providers, to survive in the market, must compete with the BBC. Thus, Independent Television News (ITN) differs from the BBC in its style and presentation but must match the latter's reputation for impartiality. ITN's commercial status frees it from some of the statutory obligations on the BBC (during coverage of general elections, for example, ITN may choose not to follow the regulatory guidelines on balance too precisely), but it adheres to public service conventions of news production because, to compete successfully, it must, as must any other serious news provider in British broadcasting.

Conversely, the BBC, although not bound by commercial constraints, must compete for audience share with the commercial news providers. Winning the case for a real increase in its licence fee

income year after year means, among other things, demonstrating its
popularity with and acceptance by the British public as a whole, who
pay the fee. In this sense, then, quasi-commercial criteria of audience
share influence the output of the public service broadcaster, which
can no longer be isolated from the market. As the broadcast journalism industry continues to expand, providers proliferate, and audiences fragment into advertiser-friendly 'niches', such pressures on the
remaining public service and state-owned broadcasters throughout
the capitalist world will increase.

Commodification and its critics

The steady commercialisation and commodification of first print and
then broadcast journalism since the mid-nineteenth century has been
accompanied by the growth of a large and dynamic news industry.
Information has become a key strategic resource, and its processed
form – journalism – a product of great political, cultural and economic significance, as we have seen. In the process, however, the style
and content of journalism has changed in accordance with the needs
and demands (real and presumed) of audiences. For many observers,
these changes have been damaging in their social effects (Bourdieu,
1998). The modern form of journalism emerged, as Chapter 2
asserted, as a *service* to democracy, a means of publicising important
information, overseeing government and political authority and per-
mitting public debate (by constituting a public sphere). These principles were formulated nearly 300 years ago and have remained in place
as a central part of liberal democratic societies. Capitalism has developed in that period, however, as has journalism, and not always, it is
argued, in a manner compatible with the principles outlined above.
What have 'Freddie Starr ate my hamster', or 'Headless body found
in topless bar',[3] to recall two notorious examples of what I have elsewhere called 'bonk' journalism (McNair, 1996), got to do with the
noble history and normative ideals of the 'fourth estate'? Not very
much, at first glance. Those who are critical of the commercialisation
of journalism will cite these as exemplars of the degeneration of the
liberal journalistic tradition and its absorption by market-driven principles of entertainment rather than information. This trend, moreover, is interpreted by some as the implementation of a broad strategy
of mass manipulation by the capitalist media, made necessary by the
advent of universal suffrage and literacy in the nineteenth century.

In early capitalism, we recall, journalism was not an item of mass consumption but an elite luxury, serving an elite public (only men of a certain educational and financial status had voting rights, and only they generally had access to and could read newspapers). As the progressive tendencies of capitalism generated mass literacy, and pressure for citizenship rights to be extended to the middle and (even!) the working classes, newspaper readerships grew and press content began to reflect the developing agenda of social reform. Titles such as *The Workingman's Friend*, *The Poor Man's Guardian* and *The Leveller* reveal the left–radical emphases of these media, an agenda which was correctly perceived as a political threat by elites in Europe and the United States.

James Curran and Jean Seaton (1997) and Michael Schudson (1978) are among those authors who have drawn attention to the fate of the nineteenth-century radical press, in both the United States and Britain, as they were driven out of an increasingly competitive, capital-intensive newspaper market by the emerging 'media barons'. Where the radical press had covered controversial political issues of reform and revolution, servicing a growing mass public newly equipped with political rights and an appetite for the information required to make use of them, the commercial press which gradually replaced them tended to avoid 'serious' matters in favour of what we would today call 'tabloid' news: crime, sex, scandal and whimsy. This, it seems reasonable to conclude from such contemporaneous remarks as the following by Lord Henry Brougham in the 1830s, was at least in part the result of a conscious strategy of social control and political management:

> It is no longer a question of whether the people shall be politicians, and take part in the discussions of their own interests, or not; that is decided long ago. The only question to answer, and the only problem to solve is, how they shall be instructed politically, and have political habits formed the most safe for the constitution of the country and the best for their own interest. (quoted in Schiller, 1981, p. 75)

From the mid-nineteenth century onwards popular journalism played an important role in the incorporation of the newly enfranchised masses into the capitalist system. The expansion of the audience for journalism was, therefore, accompanied by the deradicalisation of its content. Habermas notes that in Europe as a whole:

The mass press was based on the commercialisation of [mass] participation in the public sphere . . . [and] designed predominantly to give the masses in general access to the public sphere. This expanded public sphere, however, lost its political character to the extent that [it] could become an end in itself for a commercially fostered consumer attitude. In the case of the early penny press it could already be observed how it paid for the maximisation of its sales with the depoliticisation of its content. (1989, p. 169)

In the latter part of the nineteenth century, as literacy grew and working-class radicalism declined after several defeats in Europe, newspapers went mass-market. Competition for audiences and market share intensified. This meant the emergence of a popular press in which political and social concerns were replaced with a news diet heavily dependent on sensationalism, scandal and trivia – the staples of the popular press to this day. Anthony Sampson argues that 'as the mass market developed, the press owners assumed less and less intelligence' (1996, p. 43) on the part of their readers. This 'dumbing-down' of the press was combined, as already noted, with a strong editorial commitment to right-wing politics, enforced by proprietors who had no illusions about their role in the maintenance of the *status quo*.

Popular journalism and democracy

For more than 100 years the prevalence within popular journalism of a superficially apolitical, entertainment-led news agenda, usually framed within the context of right-wing editorial policy, has raised concerns about the role of the press in democracy. If, as has been suggested, newspapers are deemed essential to the liberal ideal of well-informed citizens acting rationally in democratic contexts, what happens if their content is dominated by coverage of sex scandals, crime and bizarre happenings of various kinds? The debate began in the late nineteenth century but has continued throughout the twentieth century, as commercial pressures have driven newspapers to be ever more prurient and sensationalist. The information, education and publicity functions of the press have, it is argued by some critics, been diluted to a pale shadow of their ideals.

The period since 1969 and Rupert Murdoch's arrival in Britain is often viewed as a particularly dark chapter in this process. Murdoch bought the *Sun*, which had until then been a moderately successful left-of-centre tabloid, and almost immediately bought the serialisation rights to Christine Keeler's biography, thus reviving the Profumo scandal of a few years earlier and earning himself in the process the nickname of the 'Dirty Digger'. Then he introduced the device of the 'page 3 girl', accompanying it with an editorial focus on sex which was unprecedented in British popular journalism. His titles also introduced aggressive marketing techniques to the promotion of the press, using bingo, television advertising and other devices new to the British scene to attract readers. In 1978, with this heady mix of sex, scandal and promotional give-aways, the *Sun* overtook the *Daily Mirror* in circulation figures and has remained the dominant tabloid ever since. In the late 1970s, as was noted earlier, it came out behind Margaret Thatcher, championing her right-wing policies in domestic and foreign affairs. For the 11 years of her period in office, the *Sun* was, it may be argued, the 'public voice' of Thatcherism.

The *Sun*'s defence against charges of prurience and political propagandising has always been precisely that it *is* popular journalism, reflecting the views of the mainly working-class people who read it. And if the liberal intelligentsia do not like it, that is their problem. The public gets what the public wants, and the *Sun* is there to give them it. The author of an affectionate and light-hearted history of the title notes that:

> Intellectuals find it beneath contempt, dismissing it as a tit-and-bum comic, not designed to be read. Attacking the *Sun* is a popular sport among those who proudly boast that they don't read it themselves – a fact that somewhat weakens their argument. But the *Sun* is not written for *Guardian* readers or eggheads who enjoy delicate debate. Its whole style is based on telling readers what they think – reflecting what is being said in pubs, on factory floors, in bus queues, behind counters and over back fences throughout the land. (Grose, 1989, p. 7)

The intellectuals who find the *Sun* 'beneath contempt', on the other hand (and there are many, even in the aftermath of the title's epoch-making decision to support Tony Blair and the Labour Party in the 1997 British general election) see it, and the tabloids in general, as the purveyors of something akin to journalistic pornography, exposing that which should remain hidden in order to generate an arousal in the reader which is almost sexual (many of the stories are sexually explicit in any case).

The *Sun*'s 'soaraway' success prompted new players to enter the British tabloid market with even more sensationalist content (the *Daily Star* in 1978, the *Daily Sport* in 1986), and existing rivals such as the *Daily Mirror* to go downmarket in a spiral of declining standards and prurience. For this reason, leading left-wing journalist John Pilger is among those who have accused Rupert Murdoch of accelerating the decline of an 'authentic' popular press (and the *Mirror*, in particular, for which Pilger had once worked). In a television documentary broadcast in 1997 he argued that, until the 1970s, the *Mirror* alone in the British tabloid market had preserved the authentically radical tradition of popular journalism, campaigning on behalf of ordinary people and against the establishment. Its decline in the 1970s and 1980s, he argued, was part of 'a wider malaise that is now so serious it threatens to sever the link between democracy and popular journalism' (1997).

The then editor of the *Mirror*, Piers Morgan, replied in a *Guardian* piece that Pilger's argument was self-serving and pompous, that the *Mirror* had been just as trivial in the 1960s and 1970s as it was accused of being in the 1990s, that there had been no golden age of campaigning popular journalism and that trivia and titillation were just as much a part of the 1960s *Mirror* as they were of the current version. The *Mirror* went into circulation decline, Morgan insisted, because people had stopped buying it. It had had to update and change, or go under, whether Pilger liked it or not (Morgan, 1997).

Some academic commentators have found sympathy with this view, interpreting the tabloidisation of news as a cultural expression of democratic development, insofar as it has indeed reflected the interests and priorities (populist and trivial though they may be) of the contemporary mass public. John Hartley, for example, argues that 'In communicating public truths (and virtue) to a post-revolutionary public, contemporary commercial journalism mixes seduction with reason, pop with politics, commerce with communication, as it has done since 1789, in the very service of public-sphere virtues' (1996, p. 201). A mass public sphere is by definition a populist public sphere in which commercial criteria play a key role. But precisely because they are bound by the rules of commerce to win audiences popular newspapers can often play a subversive political role. Hartley points out that, in their coverage of the royal family, the British tabloid press have been pro-democratic, because they so crudely expose the contradictions of primogeniture. This, he suggests, harks back to the radical origins of journalism in the struggle against feudalism, even if the primary contemporary motivation for such coverage is economic (competition). 'Those overheated but under-rated journalistic watchdogs worry and tug incessantly at the most fundamental problem that the incomplete revolution has bequeathed to the British political system – its royal family' (1996, p. 11). If the British monarchy loses what remains of its power and prestige in the coming years – and that possibility is a very real one – it will arguably be largely due to the tabloid newspapers' (and some of the broadsheets') exposure of its members as humanly fallible and imperfect.

And the tabloids 'worry and tug' not just at the remnants of Britain's feudal monarchy but at elite-group 'deviants' in general. Government ministers in extramarital affairs, heterosexual and homosexual; drug abuse by sport and entertainment celebrities; 'fat cat' businesspeople; sex-mad clergy – all have featured prominently in the British tabloid press in the 1990s. Although the views articulated in such coverage are hardly revolutionary (in the full Marxist sense of the term) they could hardly do less than encourage a disbelieving, politically cynical citizen, who justifiably takes the claims of the powerful with a pinch of salt. This may be a good or a bad thing, depending on whether one thinks the elites of capitalist society should be allowed to get on with their privileged lives in peace or be exposed and held accountable when they are corrupt, dishonest or hypocritical.

Desirable or not, it is beyond dispute that the British popular press *were* largely responsible for the wave of damaging sex and financial scandal stories which engulfed the Conservative Party after 1992 and for the steady decline in the royal family's fortunes. The modern tabloids – often owned by foreign businesspeople who are not part of the British 'establishment' – are no respecters of elite status or class. The competitive pressures of the market often push the tabloids towards positions which would be defined as subversive by the most dogmatic Marxist. For all these reasons, popular, populist journalism *can* be anti-establishment as well as sexist, racist and homophobic. Popular journalism is, in the end, a contradictory discourse, reflecting the reactionary content of popular attitudes as well as their anti-establishment prejudices.

Journalism of this type is a peculiarly British phenomenon, although other countries have their imitators. In the United States the tabloids have declined, to be replaced by *National Enquirer* type publications, described by one observer as 'bizarre hybrids which combine magazine layout and design with investigative newsgathering techniques' (Taylor, 1991, p. 17). Perhaps surprisingly, this writer regrets the passing of a truly 'tabloid' newspaper culture in the United States, and with it a democratising irreverence towards elites: 'The lesson from America is that, without the tabloids and their spirit of irreverence, the press becomes a bastion of conformity dedicated to lofty purposes understood only by the few, an instrument for and by the elite' (p. 18).

The investigative tradition

Upmarket of the tabloids, the broadsheets maintain an older tradition of critical, investigative, expository journalism, more recognisable as a 'fourth estate' overseeing standards of public life and the elite's misbehaviour. But they too have been obliged to respond to the demands of an increasingly competitive market, and an increasingly affluent, lifestyle-orientated readership.[4]

In the United States there has been the coverage of Watergate, Irangate, the Whitewater and Monica Lewinsky scandals and other instances of journalists revealing the murky undercurrents of government. In Britain the freeing of the Guildford Four, the Birmingham Six and the Bridgewater Three were all the outcome not just of dedicated legal teams but of persistent campaigning journalism over many years. In 1997 the *Daily Mail* deserved praise, in the eyes of some observers, for its revealing of the names of the alleged (but unprosecuted) killers of Stephen Lawrence. Writing in the *Guardian*, Roy Greenslade noted that this exposure would have positive effects on the campaign to put the accused behind bars. As he put it, 'Gather round, you seen-it-all before hacks and revel in the rightful use of media power to free the innocent and jail the guilty. Amid the celebrity interviews and royal tittle-tattle, this is a reason to celebrate real journalism (1997b).

Possibly the most dramatic and politically influential recent example of 'real' journalism has, however, been the campaign conducted by the *Guardian* against the corruption of standards in public life by members of parliament (MPs). Following an initial story published in October 1994 the *Guardian* (and, to a lesser extent, the *Sunday Times*) pursued the issue of 'cash for questions' for nearly three years, exposing several Conservative MPs who had taken sums of money or other favours (free accomodation at the Hotel Ritz in Paris, for example) in return for asking official questions in the House of Commons. This 'selling' of parliament's privileges and resources to the lobbying industry was not necessarily illegal but breached accepted standards of integrity in public life. The *Guardian*'s journalism led to the resignation of several MPs, two high-profile but unsuccessful libel cases (initiated by Neil Hamilton and Jonathan Aitken) and, many would argue, the defeat of the Conservative government in May 1997. The story changed the British political landscape, as Watergate had changed the US political landscape 25 years earlier, and serves as a paradigm illustration of what the media's 'fourth estate' function is supposed to be, and still can be, about.[5]

The tabloidisation of television journalism and the trivialisation of the public sphere

The power of the market is clearly seen in the press, where private ownership has always been dominant. It has been less evident in the content of broadcast journalism even where, as in the United States, private ownership of television and radio channels is the norm, because it has been perceived that broadcasters should operate by stricter standards of impartiality; that they should be positioned above the cut and thrust of party political polemicising, press editorialising and demagogery. Broadcasters, it has usually been agreed, are too important to be monopolised by one party or another but should report all credible views to a high standard of objectivity, reliability and aesthetic quality. These broad principles of broadcast journalism have been interpreted and implemented differently between systems but they form a normative standard which liberal democratic capitalist societies generally adhere to. However, as the broadcasting market has developed in the second half of the twentieth century – in particular, as it has been commercialised to an ever greater extent – the content of its journalism has come under attack.

Broadcast style

Many variants of these criticisms exist in the literature, but one strand can be summarised in the claim that, for reasons of commerce, technology and professional vanity, the style of journalism has gradually come to take precedence over substance. An increased concern with news style at the expense of substantive content is a feature observed by many critics, in both Britain and the United States. In 1994 BBC television began broadcasting a 'spoof' news programme called *The Day Today*. As its title hinted, the programme was based on a sustained lampooning of the codes and conventions of television journalism: the style of presenters and reporters; the use of sources and experts; the employment of statistics and graphics to convey trends. For journalist and culture analyst Bryan Appleyard *The Day Today* cruelly captured the fact that 'television news has become fantastically mannered and stylised. It is encrusted with gesture and posture, most of which is intended to reinforce – though in reality it subverts – its aspiration to cool objectivity and authority' (1994). This is a US-driven phenomenon, he asserts, spread by communication consultants such as Frank Magid Associates which stress the importance of presenter–anchor chemistry and personality. The goal of these stylistic developments is, in a crowded news market, to 'cultivate and advertise seriousness': 'The cult of seriousness has become a style in itself . . . there has been an extraordinary blooming of technical and representational style, driven by a highly competitive market that demands the maximum impression of significance and sensation' (Appleyard, 1994).

Broadcast news outlets have to signal difference from their competitors, and style is one means by which this can be done. The style of ITN in Britain is, as Chapter 4 noted, different from that of the BBC – 'lighter' and more informal, though still aspiring to be serious and relevant, as it must be to compete with the BBC. This does not necessarily make it inferior, unless one assumes that there is only one style of broadcast journalism which is consistent with the concept of high quality. As the market for news expands and fragments, style becomes a more important element of each provider's unique selling proposition. Different market segments require and are at ease with different styles, which is perhaps as it should be, although one observer believes that 'the [journalistic] obsession with surface is doing deep and permanent damage to the best broadcast journalism in the world' (Pearson, 1994).

'Infotainment'

Another category of criticism concerns the impact of commercial pressures on the broadcast news agenda. As the quantity of broad-

cast journalism available to viewers and listeners has grown expo-
nentially, and competition for viewers and listeners has increased,
critics argue, its agenda has followed the tabloid newspapers downmarket. The US journalist Walter Cronkite, for example, has
attacked what he sees as 'the trend towards trivialising "infotainment"' in US television news (1997), a trend he believes to be the
consequence of news organisations transforming themselves from
network loss leaders to profit centres in the 1980s. As broadcast
news has moved from being a public service to a commercial one –
the delivery of audiences to advertisers – news values are undergoing change, becoming more like those of the tabloids described
above.

Cronkite's reference was to the United States, but his argument
applies also to Britain where, too, television news has become more
focused on commercial success as measured by audience share. The
1990 Broadcasting Act required ITN to become a profit centre, with
shareholders to whom, for the first time, it became accountable.
Professional marketing and communication consultants were
employed to package and 'brand' news, and the BBC followed suit
with branding of its own. The news values of 'infotainment' were
imported from the more popular end of the newspaper market, leading Channel 4 news presenter Jon Snow to argue in 1997 that 'the
whole fabric of democracy is threatened': 'Democracy pleads that
quality news and public service information must be safeguarded –
partly through regulation and partly through being divorced from
the demand to make profit'.

Walter Cronkite (1997) agrees that high quality news and current
affairs, of the type he now believes to be under threat, is 'fundamental to the nation's welfare'. But what is 'quality' in this context, and
who defines it?

In the comments of both Snow and Cronkite we see the question-
able assumption that 'quality' equates to a particular set of news
values, a particular style and presentation of the world which focuses
on the worthy issues of politics, economic and foreign affairs, while
paying less attention to the unworthy concerns of human interest and
trivia. The Snow–Cronkite line can be viewed as an intellectual elitism which ignores the realities of the contemporary mass media audience. Not everyone in that audience wants, needs or can assimilate
'serious' news in the style deemed 'fundamental' by Cronkite. For
some, the genres of 'true crime', real-life rescue and celebrity lifestyle
coverage are as much broadcast journalism as is needed, with per-

haps a cursory scrutiny of the main news headlines to keep abreast of current events.

It may be unwelcome to some, but it seems inevitable that as broadcasting becomes more like print in its financing and market structure the news values of popular print journalism will be further replicated in television and radio. We can interpret this trend as a degradation of the public sphere, or the degeneration of journalistic principles; or we may choose to acknowledge that the 'tabloidisation' of broadcast journalism is no more nor less than one consequence of mass democracy, with positive and negative features. One observer attacks the elitism of some critics by noting that: 'Tabloid TV news simply means news led by the audience's interests – less pompous, less pedagogic, less male; more human, more vivacious, more demotic' (Dugdale, 1995). And, like tabloid newspapers, tabloid television has in places a subversive, anarchic quality which is profoundly disturbing to the establishment. In January 1997 ITV broadcast a lengthy live debate programme on the future of the British monarchy, culminating in a telephone poll showing considerable lack of support for Prince Charles as future king and a general dissatisfaction with the royal family's performance of its role. The programme shocked and disturbed many commentators with the critical savagery and lack of deference of its participants – ordinary people who were no longer passive dupes to the mythology of the Windsors.

Jon Snow, Walter Cronkite and others are, of course, entirely right to argue that quality news about politics, economics and other 'serious' matters is crucial to democracy and must be preserved in some form, but there is no serious evidence that it is in decline. BBC television produced, as of 1995, six and a half hours of news and analysis daily; ITV and Channel 4 produced another four hours; Radio 4 six hours; and Sky News and Radio 5 Live were both producing round-the-clock broadcast journalism. In November 1997 the BBC launched a 24-hour news service for the domestic market. Comparable quantities of airtime are devoted to journalism in the United States and other advanced capitalist countries.

Some of this material is 'tabloid', much more is not. The nature of the mass audience means that there is a demand for both. And as the broadcasting market fragments further under the influence of new communication technologies the scope for providing a diverse range of broadcast news styles and contents will increase, enabling all preferences to be satisfied. 'Quality', or 'serious', broadcast journalism will survive, like the broadsheet newspapers, for as long as there are people who want to watch or listen to it.

The real economic threat to journalistic quality is not in 'tabloidisation', therefore, but in the potential effect of the proliferation of organisations, and the reduction of audience share, on the resources available to each. New technology allows greater pluralism and diversity in news provision but reduces the resources available to any single producer, thus threatening quality. As Walter Cronkite puts it:

> As for the hundreds of special interests that, in the future, will supply programming for the multitude of satellite or cable channels or news sites on the Internet, it is unlikely that they will have the resources or the will to provide highly expensive, well-rounded, comprehensive news services. (1997)

Conclusions

This chapter has argued that the influence of economic factors on journalism is less predictable than we might imagine. Ownership and control give proprietors outlets through which to pursue their political agendas, of that there is no doubt, but they cannot buck market trends or ignore the views of their audience. They may try to change or influence those views (with no guarantees of success), but not to the point of putting their businesses at risk. Sometimes, as in mid-1990s Britain, they must follow their readers, in this instance as they move to the left.

Journalistic organisations have changed, it is true, from being agents of radical reform and revolution as they were in the seventeenth and eighteenth centuries, to being essentially business organisations, working in capitalist business environments. For that reason, freedom of the media has come to mean in practice, as Ralph Miliband put it many years ago, 'the free expression of ideas and opinions which are helpful to the prevailing system of power and privilege ' (1973, p. 197). If this is true as a generality we must also recognise that liberal journalism's essentially conservative function is often in conflict with the competitive demands of the media marketplace, which reward (with increased circulation and profit) exposure and revelation, particularly of the powerful. This leads to one of the most interesting features of journalism in contemporary capitalist societies and should warn us against overly simplistic denunciations of media 'bias'. Modern media 'barons' have to reconcile the political and ideological functions of journalism (and who will deny that these are essentially conservative institutions?) with their need to survive and prosper as businesses, selling news as a commodity to a public increasingly used to publicity. This leads, in many cases, to some surprisingly 'subversive' journalism. This chapter has examined how the demands of the marketplace have driven the content of newspapers and broadcast journalism towards more expository, revelatory, forms of coverage, often to the point where it can indeed be described as 'subversive' if not necessarily 'antisystemic'.

The abolition of the British royal family (to which, if it ever happens, the capitalist press will have contributed substantially) would not threaten British capitalism and might even revitalise it in some ways. Neither does the destruction by the press of the Tory Party's moral reputation threaten capitalism if the alternative is New Labour (which merely wants, in the Old Labour tradition, more efficient capitalism with a more human face). Indeed, for a moral conservative such as Rupert Murdoch, avowed Christian Tony Blair's moral agenda might seem genuinely attractive. What we have seen in Britain, it might be argued, is merely the rotation of the political elite, after 18 years, in which the Tory establishment has been relieved of its executive management of British capitalism. We can be reasonably sure that if Murdoch and the other proprietors sense the mood of their readers swinging away again, perhaps back to the Tories, they will follow suit.

|7|

The technological environment

Our starting point in this chapter is to state that the form and content of journalism is crucially determined by the available technology of newsgathering, production and dissemination available. News content is (at least in part) the outcome of the technical conditions of journalistic production. Many of these conditions are reflected in the day-to-day organisation of the newsroom (see Chapter 4), but also have relevance on the grander sociological scale, shaping the social role and function of journalism as new information and communication technologies (NICTS) create the possibility of new relationships between journalist and audience.

Not all of these developing possibilities are universally welcomed, as we shall see. New communications technology brings with it major benefits for journalistic organisations, but can also force unsettling changes on working practices and routines, challenge existing lines of demarcation in the journalistic workplace and thus easily come to be seen as a threat by practitioners. As is common in any production process, the introduction of new technology into journalism may be viewed as a blessing or a curse, depending on its implications for one's place in that process.

New communication technologies also have, as we shall see, implications for the maintenance and exercise of political authority, which many observers view as negative. The anarchic effects of new technologies such as the Internet are a central cause of the tendency towards destabilising information flows which was identified as a feature of contemporary capitalism in Chapter 2.

In exploring these issues, it is not my intention in this chapter to expound in great detail on the technical history of journalistic media but rather to identify the key historical trends underpinning specific technical innovations and then assess their sociological impact. The most significant of these, I would suggest, has been the tendency for the gap between an event taking place and its being reported to decrease.

The collapse of time–space barriers

The first 'correspondents' of early mercantile capitalism, writing their letters and sending them overland by horse and carriage, could expect weeks, even months, to elapse between their production of 'the news' and its reception by an audience back home. When news of the battle reached home the battle, as well as the war, was probably over. Gradually, over the centuries, as printing was invented and became widespread, allowing multiple copies of news-carrying texts to be made, and as transport and communication links were slowly improved, the temporal gap between an event's happening and its becoming known to a remote audience was reduced. With each new development in the means of communication the world was becoming smaller, more visible and accessible to the news audience.

Each new technological development – the telegraph and photography in the nineteenth century, the telephone in the twentieth century and film, video and digital means of information transmission in the late twentieth century – has further reduced that time–space barrier by making communication steadily quicker and easier. After the Second World War the invention of satellite communication in the 1950s made 'live' television news possible for the first time – viewers in one country could watch and learn about things happening in another part of the world, *as they were happening.*

Now, as we pass from one millenium into another, *real-time news* – instantaneous coverage of events which are taking place at the same time as they are being reported – has become a routine element of journalistic production. Immediacy in newsgathering and dissemination has become the expectation. Immediacy, indeed, has been elevated to a production goal in itself, often superseding the older and more traditional journalistic objective of contextualising and explaining the events being reported.

Technology and the dilution of content

There is a common tendency, seen both in those who run the journalistic organisations and in those who merely observe and analyse, to believe that the disappearance of the time–space 'lag' and the ascendancy of real-time news has benefited the consumer-citizen, who can thus receive information about the world sooner rather than later. In an increasingly competitive journalistic marketplace, however, the technological possibilities of real-time news have also had the effect of reducing the time available to journalists for editorial decision-making. News is more simultaneous, and there is more of it, but it is at the same time more 'bitty' and unrefined. New technology, in other words, accentuates the tendency towards event-orientated coverage identified in Chapter 4, threatening the depth and thus, one could argue, the quality of information provided. Combined with the effects of the market which we have already examined, technology encourages the producers of news to aspire to ever more immediacy and instantaneity. Being there, and being there *first*, becomes a goal in itself, regardless of whether one has anything of value to say journalistically, leading to what Brent MacGregor calls 'knee jerk grandstanding' (1997) by journalists.

Once the information is processed (gathered on portable video, edited on a portable editing suite in the hotel room and transferred to head office by satellite in time for the next bulletin) it can join the competition for access to the public sphere with all the other 'bits' constantly coming in. Computer-aided design and graphics allow it to be quickly worked up into an apparently seamless account of what really happened 'out there'. And as these possibilities emerge, they tend to become standard – their routine implementation a necessity for any 'serious' news organisation. As Ivor Yorke puts it, 'real-time television – live or very recently recorded pictures beamed back by satellite – has created a new grammar and editorial agenda for TV news coverage, bringing with it fresh dynamics and pressures' (1995, p. 6).

One leading British journalist, himself the anchor on a highly respected, hi-tech news bulletin (*Channel 4 News*), argues that 'the technology [of modern news production] enables us to package, graphicise and meld five minutes of old TV information into 60 seconds of new TV time – the whizz and bang of such presentation may be enticing but the content reduction is so acute that normal debate is in danger of being degraded to the absurd' (Snow, 1997). Just as the commercial pressures on journalists to make 'infotainment' (Chapter 6) are alleged to undermine the core aims of journalism (to inform, educate and facilitate rational public debate) so too the pernicious effects of the often dazzling new technological possibilities may lead journalists to lose sight of what it is they are supposed to be doing in the first place. New technology, from this point of view, reinforces the trend towards 'style over substance'.

As was noted in an earlier discussion of style, however, this view is debatable, imposing as it does one essentially subjective aesthetic judgment of what news *should* be on an industry which is undergoing almost permanent revolution. Real-time news and the innovations in style and presentation which new technology allows (computer graphics, virtual reality newsrooms, etc.) are not replacements for some earlier, superior form of news – they *add* to a news market which contains somewhere, in the broadsheet newspapers or among the hundreds of hours of broadcast news and current affairs which make up the schedules in countries such as the United States and Britain, all the 'normal debate' one could wish for. One only has to watch the pioneering television news bulletins of the 1950s to see how much the gathering, production and presentation of information has improved, aided by technological innovation. Television news was never all that information-rich, if compared with other media such as radio and print, and it has certainly not become more so over time. On the other hand, as we shall see below, new distributive technologies such as digitalisation and the Internet have made possible a broader range of journalistic outlets and a flourishing of varied styles which may go some way to addressing the concerns expressed by Snow.

Real-time news and the political process

Another effect of the technology-driven collapse of time–space barriers in journalism, it is often argued, is political. Chapter 5 alluded to the fact that as information in the form of news and journalism becomes more immediate, more intimate and more *public,* the political environment within which our governors must make decisions is complicated by a new factor. Information, and its impact on audiences, becomes an important variable in the equations politicians must draw up when deciding policy matters.

This consequence of technological innovation has both positive and negative aspects. In relation to the former, it can be argued that anything which reduces the power of political elites to ignore or subvent popular, democratic processes is a good thing. Information is a power resource, and politicians have always sought to control, manage and manipulate it for their own ends. Throughout most of human history, moreover, they have been able to do so largely unhindered. No more.

The attempted coup of August 1991 in Moscow, which would have returned Europe and the world to the ideological polarities and tensions of the cold war had it been successful, failed largely because it was reported on television, communicated by fax and e-mail and because there was a strong enough civil society in place – five years after Mikhail Gorbachev had begun his historic reforms – to take advantage of that openness and transparency. The Moscow coup unfolded in the media, and failed there, watched by millions within the Soviet Union and abroad. Journalism on its own did not cause the coup to fail, but tipped the balance just far enough in favour of the popular will to make its failure inevitable.

In China's Tienanmen Square, on the other hand, the presence of news teams at the 1989 pro-democracy demonstrations did not prevent the bloody massacre which transpired. It ensured, however, that the brutality of the Chinese regime was revealed to the world, with real consequences for China's place in the global community which are still being felt by its rulers. The newsgathering possibilites created by video and satellite technology meant that this crime could not be committed in secrecy but was witnessed by the whole world through the medium of television journalism.

In short, the immediacy and 'liveness' of contemporary broadcast journalism has altered the nature of the relationship between those who wield political power and those over whom, or in whose name, it is wielded; a shift which this author, for one, wholeheartedly welcomes. Control of information, or its denial, or restriction of the rights of journalists to do their jobs, through censorship, secrecy or other means, enhances power. Failure to deny information subverts power. In this sense, as the Soviet coup plotters found out in 1991, the 'information society' makes despotism impossible, or at least much more difficult, and makes democracy much more likely in the long run (China will be a test case of this in the twenty-first century). News gets out. Power, and the abuse of power, are on public display to an extent unprecedented in human history.

But there are those who bemoan this new journalistic environment, arguing that it subverts the ability of governors to govern well, which is of course not something any but the anarchists among us would wish for. Politicians, as already noted, wish to control information flows, not just in the interests of self-preservation but in the name of good government. Sometimes, discretion and reflection are required in the political decision-making process, for the good of society as a whole. As British television journalist Nik Gowing (1994) has argued, coolness, confidentiality and control in relation to information are often, if not always, in the public interest. Contemporary political crises can be immensely complex, requiring great diplomatic and political sensitivity if they are to be resolved with optimal benefit for all concerned. In the post-cold war world of ethnic conflict, where problems are often rooted in obscure historical events, politicians more than ever require the time and the space to think, consult, reflect and decide. Controlling the flow of information is central to providing this opportunity.

Now, however, politicians' control of information flows is constantly challenged by the complicating factor of real-time news and a journalistic culture which often places immediacy of coverage over analytical depth or reflection. Politicians who might once have taken the time to make considered decisions on domestic or foreign affairs now find themselves 'bounced' into taking action, or at the very least being seen to be taken action. Such considerations of public presentation were behind the US government's dispatch of troops to Somalia in 1995, a military expedition which began well, live on television, but ended in humiliation and retreat because it was not a good decision. Throughout the conflict in the former Yugoslavia, Western governments based their responses as much on calculations of how those responses would impact on public opinion, which was responding to images consumed through the media, as on rational decisions about what might be the best policy.

One should not blame our politicians for their desire to receive positive coverage of their policy decisions and actions. Their electorates have shown more than once that they will punish those who fail by this test. But it leads, inevitably, to a less rational, more public relations-orientated approach to policy formulation. We live, as a consequence, in an age of reflexive decision-making (politicians and other elites make decisions in the context of receiving more and more information, more and more rapidly, about themselves, through the journalistic media, via opinion polls, market research and so on). This encourages the *chaotic* pattern of interaction between media organisations and decision-makers discussed in Chapter 2. NICTs increase the possibilities of democratic participation, but the speed of contemporary information dissemination reduces the time available for the processing and analysis of raw data. This makes governments (and decision-makers generally) vulnerable, increasing their tendency to secrecy and disinformation, and reducing democratic control.

From control to chaos

The collapse of time–space barriers in the production of journalism thus encourages the related trend of a deterioration in the ability of political elites (and indeed other elites, in business, the military, the cultural world) to control their decision-making environment and an increase in the unpredictability and chaos which accompanies the governing process. Just as the speed of modern newsmaking and dissemination makes journalism itself an increasingly frantic and unrehearsed activity, so those who must take journalism into account when making decisions are more vulnerable to poor decision-making. This can be a good or a bad thing, depending on one's judgments about such matters as the ethical basis of the government's policies or the extent to which it has genuine public interests at heart. Whether good or bad in its consequences, however, no government can ignore the implications of real-time news for the formulation, presentation and execution of policy.

Globalisation

As journalism has become more immediate it has also become more global, not just in the sense of bringing events in the wider world 'home' to individual members of the audience, but also in making the audience itself more international and 'global' in nature. The twenty-first century, to a far greater extent than has been the case in the latter years of the twentieth, will be the era of the global news broadcaster (print, not least because of language constraints, will remain localised in its reach), and indeed analysts of journalism are now witnessing a struggle for global domination between a handful of key players in this huge and potentially very lucrative market.

There have been global broadcasters since the Second World War, of course. 'News' organisations funded by the United States, Soviet and other governments used radio to transmit propaganda around the world in the battle for ideological supremacy. These, however, were propaganda organs, recognised and often discounted as such by those to whom they broadcast. Radio Free Europe, Voice of America,

Moscow Radio and their equivalents in France, China and elsewhere were not taken seriously as journalistic organisations. Only the BBC, with its World Service, combined an international audience with a reputation for objectivity and political independence which allowed it to avoid the charge of propaganda. Perhaps most famously, when Mikhail Gorbachev was being held under house arrest by the coup leaders of 1991, he (by his own account) relied on the World Service for accurate and objective reports of what was going on in Moscow.

The era of global television (as opposed to radio) journalism began on June 1 1980, when US entrepreneur Ted Turner launched his Cable News Network (CNN). Turner's idea of a 24-hour cable news channel, distributed by satellite across the United States, was the beginning of what has been called a 'second age' of television in which, utilising technological innovation, the nature of news and information would be fundamentally transformed. In this sense, we might say that Ted Turner was the 'father' of real-time news as well as a pioneer of journalistic globalisation. By 1983 CNN's domestic operation was in profit and, having conquered the United States, Turner then shifted his attentions to the rest of the world, and to Europe in particular. From here CNN gradually expanded to become the global broadcaster 'of choice', not just for business travellers seeking a reliable up-to-date news service but also for political elites and opinion formers.

This it did on the back of two key events, which dramatically demonstrated the power of real-time news and its appeal to a global audience. In 1986 the *Challenger* spacecraft exploded on take-off in Florida. CNN's 24-hour operation allowed its cameras to be there, and on air, at the crucial moment, and thus for its pictures to be rapidly broadcast around the world. While other news broadcasters were tied to long-established slots in carefully controlled airtime, and were available only to domestic audiences, CNN could follow the story as it developed and share it with the world via satellite transmissions.

The second key event establishing CNN's pre-eminence in the global news business was the Gulf war of 1990–91. This truly global crisis was the first of its kind to be reported live, and CNN came to occupy a key role, reporting developments not just to ordinary citizens in North America, Europe or the Middle East but also to political decision-makers in their offices, who used the channel as a source of information while weighing up what to do next. Key protagonists such as Saddam Hussein proactively used CNN (and the other news media) as a means of communicating with their opposite numbers, sending out messages over the airways in the knowledge that opposing political leaders and their advisers would be sure to be watching.

CNN was the first, but by no means the last, of the new wave of global news broadcasters. CNN's commercial success inevitably attracted other entrants into the market, although none have as yet achieved the impact and name recognition enjoyed by Turner's company. Rupert Murdoch has gradually extended his satellite news services beyond Britain and the United States to span the globe, including the countries of Asia and the Pacific Rim. The BBC has built on its World Service reputation and newsgathering infrastructure, using the new communication technologies, to develop BBC World.

Cultural imperialism

Notwithstanding the technologically-driven inevitability with which journalism is globalising its output, some observers are wary of the cultural implications of large, usually US-based, multinationals coming to dominate, if not monopolise, the production of news for global audiences. In a variant of the long-heard cultural imperialism thesis, it is argued that local cultures, with their local news values and agendas, will be swamped by the largely US agendas of the emerging global broadcasters such as CNN. And this is not a concern merely of liberal cultural theorists. The Director General of the BBC, John Birt, has warned that 'the easy availability of programmes and services worldwide will encourage the emergence of a single global culture. A single global culture will mean an Americanised world culture' (1996). In the sphere of journalism, as well as in other fields of cultural production, few dispute that this, if it happens, would amount to a deterioration of the cultural environment. The threat of 'cultural imperialism' is overstated, however. CNN can be said to have created the market for global television news, but its US-dominated news agenda, shaped by the fact that its market is predominantly US, has limited its expansion in global terms. Outside of the United States, and away from the business hotels of London, Tokyo or Moscow, few actually watch CNN, unless at times of 'breaking stories' when, as was noted above, the channel has a real competitive advantage. People in Britain, France or Australia do not want to know about what is happening in the American mid-West unless, like the Oklahoma bombing, it is a genuinely global news story. Then, CNN dominates the market, as it will do for some time to come.

The experience of CNN has presented other aspiring global news organisations with the problem of how to develop a news style and agenda which is exportable to many different cultural marketplaces. The BBC's approach, for example, has been to stress its historical reputation for non-propagandistic objectivity and its avoidance of a British-dominated agenda in its international news coverage. In the regions where it operates it may tailor its programmes, as indeed does CNN. In these ways it hopes to avoid charges of 'cultural imperialism' and instead project the image of a service organisation, supplying quality journalism which is genuinely of use to many diverse markets and not a threat to indigenous values and traditions. And, in the main, the BBC has been successful in this approach. Where it has encountered opposition to its international journalism it has usually come from governments such as those of China and Saudi Arabia, where it is the political rather than cultural threats posed by independent, objective media which exercise political elites.

Global journalism is not, of course, and never should be, a substitute for the availability of quality journalism at the national level. And in many countries, including most of Europe, this means some commitment by the state to protect, on behalf of the people, existing public service channels. As John Birt has put it (he has a clear self-interest in putting this argument, but it makes sense nonetheless), 'the most effective means of countering the risks of the globalisation of culture, and declining standards will be by sustaining publicly-funded broadcasters' (1996). If this can be done, the more optimistic scenario presented by Jo Bardoel may be borne out:

> The original agitation around CNN is reminiscent of the unease that accompanies each new technological development upon which new and more direct forms of reporting are based. We may expect the new direct and global television reporting to carve itself a niche alongside – and not primarily instead of – existing forms of journalism. (1996, p. 290)

Digitalisation and the proliferation of channels

A further key trend associated with the development of new information and communication technologies has been digitalisation, and the proliferation of channels which it is producing. As the Director General of the BBC puts it:

> Our [broadcasting] world was born of spectrum scarcity, a handful of channels and regulation. The analogue technology which underpinned 70 years of British broadcasting is to give way to a brand new and different technology – digital. The impact will be seismic. (Birt, 1996)

For the production of journalism, as for televisual culture in general, digitalisation will mean: an improved quality of image and thus an ever more heightened realism in journalistic output (through such innovations as high-definition television, wide-screen television and digital stereo sound); an increasing plurality of channels, allowing for greater targetting of the audience; a new interactivity in the relationship between viewer and broadcaster; and greater access to journalism, simply because there will be much more of it around.

The full impact of these developments are still perhaps five to ten years from full fruition, but the expanding opportunities provided by the Internet already give a glimpse of the interactive, multichannel future promised by digital television.

These changes, if they come about, will probably come to be seen as a good thing by most viewers. Not everyone, for example, wants access to 24-hour news, but for those who do, CNN, News Corporation or the BBC will provide it, probably at a cost. The BBC used savings from the introduction of new technologies and consequent resource-saving strategies such as 'bi-media' (where one production crew can supply material for both radio and television news) to set up Radio 5 Live (an addition to the United Kingdom's public service provision), using that experience to develop a 24-hour news service on television, which came on-air in November 1997. There will be a cost to the viewer for this service, but as long as the existing core of public service broadcasting remains free and accessible, and given that readers of a daily newspaper will spend between £100 and £200 a year on one title, it is difficult to argue that such specialised services, likely to be most intensively used by educated, professional, relatively affluent viewers, should be free as of right.

The new technologies which are so revolutionising the quantity and quality of journalism available to the television audience of the twenty-first century will not, however, alter the basic, age-old laws of capitalist accumulation. As we saw in Chapter 6, the structure of ownership and control of journalistic media remains a key issue for audiences and legislators the world over, and the new digital environment will not change that fact. How can the domination of a very few globally active news organisations be prevented, and genuine diversity of provision, of choice, be preserved? How can the new pressures of competition which digitalisation has unleashed be prevented from leading to a further deterioration in the production resource base, leading to drops in the standard of programming?

Here again, as in the issue of cultural imperialism, the survival of existing, terrestrial broadcasters is key. Whether publicly financed (like the BBC) or commercially operated (like ITN), the continuing presence of respected 'quality' broadcast journalism in the rapidly fragmenting news marketplace will act as an incentive for the providers of the next century to maintain a level of standard which viewers of the twentieth century would recognise as acceptable. The maintenance of quality in this sense can never be guaranteed, of course, and Cronkite's warnings (see the section on 'infotainment' in Chapter 6) ought to be heeded by global media regulators, but a proliferation of providers of journalism need not mean that the cheapest will come to dominate. On the contrary, as has been seen with Sky News in Britain, rather than all channels sinking to the level of the lowest common denominator in quality terms, those who wish to be taken seriously, to acquire credibility as purveyors of news, will have to rise to the standard of the existing market leaders in each country.

The Internet and the death of print

Of all the technological developments which have driven the evolution of journalism in recent years, among the most important will surely turn out to be the transglobal network of linked computers known popularly as the Internet. This innovation, which combines the vast storage and data-processing capabilities of modern computers with the distributive power of orbiting satellites to create a truly global, practically indestructible communicative apparatus, has major implications for the practice of journalism, and its role in 'networked' societies.

The consequences of the Internet are consistent with those already examined above – the erosion of time–space barriers in the production and consumption of news; the globalisation of news and its audiences; the proliferation of outlets – but Internet technology accelerates these processes, advances them to a new stage, at which traditional journalistic media, print media in particular, are said to be in danger of becoming redundant.

The 'death of print' is an old refrain, of course, heard regularly throughout the twentieth century as film, radio, television, video, personal computers and latterly the Internet have been accused of removing the usefulness of newspapers (and indeed books). And in relation to the Internet especially we can see why this view has appeal to futurologists. As US analyst and media manager Jon Katz has put it, 'everything a newspaper used to do somebody else is doing more quickly, more attractively, more efficiently, and in a more interesting and unfettered way' (1995). As we have noted, speed of delivery of information is an important 'quality' standard of modern journalism and one which each successive technological leap has tended to highlight. From the telegraph to the Internet, the gap between news happening and information about it being delivered to audiences has shrunk until it is now virtually (in more ways than one) non-existent. Katz again:

> TV meant that breaking news could be reported quickly, colorfully, and – eventually – live. Live TV supplanted the historic function of the journalist. Cable TV meant a whole new medium with the time and room to present breaking and political news, entertainment news, live trial coverage. Computers meant that millions of people could flash the news to one another. All of these changes have given newspapers a diminished role in the presentation of news. (1995)

By way of illustration, on 28 February 1997 the *Dallas Morning News* reported Oklahoma bomber Timothy McVeigh's confession straight onto its Internet website, *before* putting it in the newspaper. This act of editorial hara-kiri represented, for one observer, 'a major step in the evolution of newspapers' (Katz, 1997); an acknowledgement by the dinosaurs of print journalism that the future lay in cyber space.

Concern about the implications of the Internet for the future of print journalism were first prompted by the Microsoft company's entry into the on-line journalism business, with *CityScope* in January 1995, an electronic publication containing news, reviews and listings which was presented as the future of news media. Since then, more and more titles have set up on-line versions of their newspapers, eager to be seen as part of the information revolution rather than standing outside of it. As of 1997 there were some 700 on-line 'newspapers' in the United States and dozens in the United Kingdom and Western Europe, with more joining the Internet all the time.

However, electronic newspapers are still at the experimental stage in their development, unsure of what they should be doing, who they are for and how they are to be used. The belief that being part of the Internet revolution is important is now common sense for most major newspapers, but this perception has not been matched by an ability to use the communicative possibilities of on-line formats. The majority of Net newspapers look like stripped-down electronic versions of their printed parents. Unlike the latter, however, you cannot just turn the page or go straight to the sports section. Using the Internet requires expensive hardware and software, telephone usage and subscriptions to Internet service providers, all adding up to a considerable investment of time and money. Having made this investment, the user may well want to see more than a heavily-truncated, poorly-designed version of a newspaper which can be bought in its old-fashioned entirety for a few cents or pence from any street-corner news vendor. Most on-line newspapers are precisely that, however.

Most of the exceptions are those titles (*Slate* is one such) which have originated with the Internet and have sought to capture the graphic and design possibilities of the computer screen, moving away from the concept of the 'electronic newspaper' towards something more akin to an easily-manipulable, multimedia, constantly-update-able database – not replacing the newspaper format but supplementing it with a medium which has the immediacy and liveness of broadcasting, while retaining the depth and space provided by print.

Even if all electronic newspapers were to become as 'readable' as *Slate*, however, those concerned about the death of the newspaper in the coming decades should recall that

- Print does things which no other medium can, and will continue to do so for some time to come.
- The invention of television did not make radio redundant; on the contrary, radio is more popular than ever. Nor has television destroyed the habit of reading books or the book publishing industry, contrary to the dire predictions of some pessimists.
- The invention of home video did not destroy the market for cinema. On the contrary, cinema audiences have increased significantly in recent years as people have become aware that the experience of watching at least some films on the big screen is something which the convenience of home video does not compensate for.

Similarly, the arrival of the Internet does not remove the rationale for (or the specific pleasures of) buying and reading newspapers – in bars and pubs over a coffee or a beer, on the metro or the bus going to work, during one's lunch break. No matter how cheap and accessible the Internet eventually becomes, it will never (at least not in this writer's lifetime) be possible to roll it up and put it in your pocket. With the Internet we will never be able to feel the paper, see the typography, get our hands black with printer's ink. As Jon Katz observes:

> Delivered to your door daily, newspapers are silent, highly portable, require neither power source nor arcane commands, and don't crash or get infected. They can be stored for days at no cost and consumed over time in small, digestible quantities. They can also be used to line trash cans and train pets. They're recyclable. (1995)

The common-sense mundanity of print's use value – its unique selling proposition – is what guarantees the medium a place in the virtual universe of the twenty-first century. Newspapers will survive precisely because they are 'lo-tech' and do not require an expensive infrastructure to be accessed. Newspapers imply what we might call a 'freedom of consumption', allowing the reader to be independent of the seductive (and expensive) information technology of the moment. The Internet has many seductions of its own, but it necessarily ties the user into being at ease with (and being able to purchase) a constantly changing supporting apparatus of modems, computer terminals and phone lines. Some years ago, before the mass communicative potential of the Internet was widely understood, a British observer noted that:

> It is the printed word, with its unlimited capacity for comprehensive investigation of a situation and the detailed unravelling of complex issues beyond the scope of the oral bulletin, its unrivalled quality as a forum in which ideas can be exchanged and pros and cons set out and argued, its durability as a record of what people say and do, its flexibility as a pocket medium that can be carried about and kept to be read and re-read at will, that in the final analysis must be the most important safeguard of the democratic process. (Baistow, 1983, p. i)

This impassioned defence of print journalism's democratic function is also an excellent list of reasons why it is less vulnerable to the Internet than some may fear.

Less obvious than the value of print as a pocket medium, or even cat litter, but of no less significance in guaranteeing a future for newspapers, is the very scope and pace of the information revolution which supposedly threatens their existence. Many observers warn of 'information overload' in connection with the proliferation of outlets which digitalisation and other technological innovations have made possible. We are in danger, it is often argued, of being overwhelmed by too much information, losing our ability to sift and sort it, to make sense of and evaluate it. If this *is* a problem (and readers may judge for themselves on the basis of their own experience) the lo-tech slowness and tactility of print may turn out to be, for many, a means of standing back from the information superhighway and taking a breather:

> The explosion of new media needn't eliminate the traditional journalistic print function. Quite the opposite, it could make newspapers more vital, necessary and useful than ever. The more complicated the gadgets become, and the more new media mushroom, the more we need what newspapers have always been – gatekeepers and wellheads, discussion leaders on politics and public policy questions. (Katz, 1995)

Individuals may 'lose their way on the information superhighway and feel a greater need for journalistic direction' (Bardoel, 1996, p. 285).

> More than ever, the task of journalism [in print and every other medium] will lie in filtering relevant issues from an increasing supply of information in a crowded domain and its fragmented segments. Journalism evolves from the provision of facts to the provision of meaning. (Bardoel, 1996, p. 297)

Fortunately, then, for those who work in print journalism, and for those (many millions in all industrialised societies) who value the opportunity to read them, reports of the death of print are premature. For the time being (if not necessarily for ever), electronic publishing does not present a major threat to the traditional print industries. On-line publications are, at present, marginal extensions of the main business of newspapers and periodicals. They demand access to expensive computer equipment and a degree of computer literacy which is by no means universal. Certainly, just as the masses learnt to read in the nineteenth century and provided the market for an explosion of popular newspapers, so in the twenty-first century more and more people will become routine users of computer technology. The technology itself will become steadily cheaper and more accessible. As it does so, on-line publications will increase in number and in readership. By the end of the first decade of the twenty-first-century who can doubt that every home will be connected to the Internet (as today every home has a television), which will have become a major resource for entertainment, education and communication? On-line publications will flourish, if only to fill the space provided by this new medium.

They will not replace newspapers, if only because newspapers can do things which websites cannot. The habit of buying and reading newspapers is unlikely to die out with the twentieth century, although newspapers will inevitably have to update their services and presentation, emphasising what it is they do that is truly unique to print and downgrading or even abandoning those elements of their traditional output which the Internet will be able to do better.

The Internet and power

In one respect, however, the impact of the Internet is unambiguous. The arrival of the Internet effectively destroys the traditional controls enjoyed by elites over information and its dissemination. For film buffs, Harry Knowles's US-based website makes available information about the cinema industry which its managers and stars would rather remained secret, or known only to a select few within the industry – commercially important information such as the response of a preview audience to a planned blockbuster movie.[1] In politics, Internet reports of the William Straw (son of Jack Straw) cannabis bust undermined the Labour government's efforts to keep the embarrassing story secret. In the United States, as the Monica Lewinsky scandal broke in January 1998 it was the Drudge Report (www.drudgereport.com) website which leaked damaging transcripts and other information. In the management of politics, as in the attempted restriction of pornography, the Internet undermines elite attempts at secrecy, and makes the free, or chaotic, flow of information into a major consideration of policy-makers and decision-takers.[2] The Internet has become, within a few short years of its emergence as a mass consumer item, a factor of growing importance in the evolution and resolution of political and other types of crisis.

Conclusion: the Internet as a new public sphere

If the Internet need not be seen as a threat to existing journalistic media, it should nevertheless be recognised as an epochal advance in human communication. Some commentators argue that the inherent interactivity and accessibility of the Internet will encourage democracy. As Jon Katz argues:

> Digital news differs radically from other media. No other medium has ever given individual people such an engaged role in the movement of information and opinion or such a proprietary interest in the medium itself. The computer news culture fosters a sense of kinship, ownership, and participation that has never existed in commercial media. (1997)

Anthony Sampson extends this line of reasoning to argue that, if traditional print media are becoming more trivial and entertainment-led (although, as we have seen, this is only one interpretation of what is happening to news content), the new technologies can create a new version of the 'coffee-house culture' of the eighteenth century (the seedbed of the public sphere), allowing us to escape from the clutches of media barons such as Murdoch, Berlusconi, Springer or Black. Says Sampson:

> The best elements of the media have always arisen from natural talk, discussion, curiosity and questions – as eighteenth century papers grew out of coffee-houses. If mass-communication has become too distorted and corrupted, it may be thought that the Internet and e-mail will provide the new technologies to rescue from the old ones, to build up more reliable systems of information across the world. (1996, p. 51)

The Internet has the potential to democratise the media, in other words, restoring (or, if you like, creating for the first time) a genuine public sphere by restoring control over the means of communication to the people. The coming years will demonstrate if this is misplaced utopianism or a realistic assessment of the liberating potential of a technology which is uniquely difficult to police and regulate, thus uniquely free from the commercialisation and elite control which have eventually subdued all other media forms in human history.

8

The sociology of sources

Previous chapters in Part II have addressed the influence on journalistic output of the political, economic and technological environments within which the individual journalist functions. In this chapter we consider a fourth extramedia factor of journalistic production and one of growing importance for the sociologist of journalism – namely, the influence of *sources* and their activities on output. Attention to this factor distinguishes what has been called the *source-centred approach* to the sociology of journalism (as opposed to media-centred or journalist-centred) and is based on the premise that both the agenda and the content of journalism are in significant part the product of the communicative work of non-journalistic social actors. As Miller and Williams have put it, 'in order to understand routine news coverage . . . it is necessary to examine the strategies formulated by sources of information to influence and use the news media' (1993, p. 3). Not just routine news coverage but the output of journalism in general is increasingly the product of activity taking place out in the world beyond the journalist's immediate working environment – communicative work which is deliberately designed and organised to shape news in ways favourable to the individual or organisation initiating it.

Such is the importance of these source activities that they have become the province of a professional group separate from, but dependent on, journalism, and known variously as the public relations practitioner; the spin doctor; the parliamentary or congressional lobbyist; the political consultant; the communications advisor; the 'media guru'. These are just some of the labels applied to the source professional, who has emerged in the twentieth century in the wake of the media's rapid expansion, feeding the latter's insatiable desire for raw material to package as news and entertainment.

The rise of a category of source professionals is the flipside of the process which has seen journalism grow in cultural significance throughout the twentieth century. As journalism has become more important, so has the perceived need on the part of decision-makers and would-be opinion formers to shape and manage it. Public relations and its related fields of expertise have not yet acquired the respectability or professional status of journalism, and its exponents are frequently demonised in the news (in Britain, Max Clifford, Ian Greer, Peter Mandelson; in the United States, Dick Morris, Richard Wirthlin) but few doubt their importance as influences on and shapers of what we experience as 'news'. They are, to quote Labour Minister Clare Short, speaking of her Party's public relations apparatus in 1996, 'the people who live in the dark';[1] somewhat sinister, yet glamorous and, for some at least, perversely attractive figures engaged in a fiercely competitive struggle with the journalists to define the terms of media coverage.

This chapter concludes our analysis of the factors involved in the manufacture of journalism by examining the techniques used by source professionals to manage and influence news, on behalf of a range of corporate, political and other organisational clients, who seek publicity and, through it, the achievement of various political objectives.

The sociology of the source professional

Public relations, news management, 'spinning', as communicative practices rather than labels, are not unique to the twentieth century but date from the establishment and the emergence of 'publics' from the eighteenth century onwards. The French political philosopher Rousseau would not have understood what the term 'public relations' means but he did nevertheless write in the nineteenth century that 'whoever makes it his business to give laws must know how to sway opinions and through them govern the passions of man' (quoted in Bloom, 1973, p. 1). In the seventeenth century King Charles II reportedly employed the services of diarist Samuel Pepys as a 'press handler' for the sum of 30 guineas.[2]

Public relations, then – which I will define for the moment as the conscious effort to 'sway opinion', as Rousseau expressed it – has been around for as long as there have been significant (that is, politically important) opinions to be swayed and media available for use

in swaying them. Only in the modern era, however, can we say that
there has been a need for individuals and organisations working in
the spheres of business or politics to sway mass *public opinion*. Only
in the twentieth century, for example, did the ordinary populations
of even the most advanced capitalist societies win full rights to vote
in free elections, regardless of property and educational qualifica-
tions, sex or ethnic background. Only then, therefore, did their opinions begin to matter politically insofar as they could for the first time
be translated into votes for or against this or that party. Before universal suffrage the opinions of the public were of no consequence
politically, as opposed to the views of the educated, male, white
bourgeois who alone could vote or stand for election.

Around the same time as ordinary people were becoming vote-
wielding citizens, the communication media were developing into
mass media as rates of literacy increased, popular newspapers
became established and news became a key element of an expanded
public sphere. It was at this point, therefore, that public relations
emerged as a distinctive specialist sphere of communicative work
aimed at influencing the journalistic content of the public sphere – a
profession distinct from print journalism and the communicative
work of political actors but intimately connected with both. The two
major developments of relevance to the sociology of sources were,
then:

- the expansion of universal suffrage
- the expansion of mass media.

The first generated a political environment in which the winning of
public opinion became a precondition for the pursuit of effective
political action (in or out of government). The second created a common media space where such efforts could be played out. Indeed, the
rapid expansion of the media created a demand for news and put
pressure on news organisations not just to sit back and report newsworthy events but to go out and find them, or, if they could not be
found, to go out and manufacture them. Thus developed a mutually
beneficial relationship between the political actor (source of news)
and the media (producers of news), mediated by the emerging public
relations industry.

As the size and representativeness of the 'public sphere' increased,
under popular pressure and the influence of key events such as the
First World War, so did the need for 'public relations' – which we can
also think of as the management of relations between the powerful

and the public. Public relations is thus a creature of the twentieth century, born of the need to link political actors' hunger for publicity with the demands of the media for journalistic raw material. Calvin Coolidge was the first US president to employ a full-time press officer, and from the early years of the twentieth century 'press counsellors', as Edward Bernays (1923) called them, were being employed to influence public opinion on behalf of US business and political organisations.[3] Quickly thereafter the practice of public relations spread to the rest of the capitalist world, with immense consequences for the way public affairs, and politics in particular, were organised and practised. As R.W. Fenton put it in 1966:

> Political scientists a few years hence may well view the introduction of 'professional public relations' into US politics as the most significant development in government since the late nineteenth century. In fact, not since the emergence of machine politics in the 1870s and the rise of the so-called 'ward boss' has there been a transition more noteworthy in the political mores of America. (p. 25)

What is true for the United States has also been true, a little later perhaps, for Britain and Western Europe, Australasia and the Far East. In fact, wherever democratic principles of government have been embraced, the necessity for systematic management of public opinion has followed as a necessary correlate. Once the members of a society have acquired the right to vote for (or against) their political leaders, the latter have a clear interest in seeking to influence how voters think and behave politically, while avoiding the charge of 'propagandist'. Corporate actors, too, faced with governments which must be seen to be responsive to public opinion, have a clear interest in mobilising public opinion behind their campaigns, or at least neutralising any hostility which might exist on, for example, environmental or regulatory issues.

That the communicative dimension of political action has expanded in this way is not just the consequence of democracy but is just as much the technology-driven product of the media's expansion and the ever-increasing opportunities which this provides for political and social actors to gain access to media space. The media are the platform from which modern political debate is conducted – with *mediation* by the journalists, of course, shaped by professional culture and practice (see Chapter 4). Public relations (or its media relations subdiscipline) is no more nor less than the set of techniques by which social actors seek to manage their appearances on that platform. They are helped in this by the fact that the media, as they have grown in range and diversity, have also expanded their appetite for raw material, their hunger for news. Without reportable stories journalism cannot function, and so the need for political actors to attempt to influence public opinion coincides with the needs of the media for material. A symbiosis develops, in which the skilful source professional can exploit the media's dependence upon him or her to gain advantage for the 'client'. The political actor's 'publicity' is at the same time the journalist's 'news'.

The state of mutual interdependence thus established between journalist and source gives the latter a degree of power over the product of journalism that no sociology can ignore. Journalism, as we have seen, is the product, to varying degrees dependent on circumstances, of aesthetic convention, political regulation and censorship, market forces, proprietorial decree, the limits of technical possibility and the rules and practices imposed by professional culture. It is also shaped by what social actors do to manage their representation in journalistic media – and they can do a great deal.

Public relations and the creation of news

One of the first public relations 'gurus', Edward Bernays, in 1923 described the work of the 'public relations counsel' thus:

> [He] . . . is a creator of news for whatever medium he chooses to transmit his ideas . . . He must isolate ideas and develop them into events so that they can be more readily understood and so that they may claim attention as news. (p. 171)

> An understanding of what news is must be an integral part of the equipment of the public relations counsel. For the public relations counsel must not only supply news – he must create news. (p. 185)

The 'creation' of news was achieved by the designing of events which would be likely to be attractive to journalists: *pseudo-events*, as Daniel Boorstin (1962) called them in the 1960s, implying by this label that such events were in some sense unreal, having no rational meaning and no point outwith the circle of the media for which they were designed. Culture critic Gilbert Adair observes that 'Pseudo-events are generated by journalistic coverage. Or, in a nutshell, events are covered by journalists because they occur, and pseudo-events occur because they are covered by journalists' (1995).

The proactive dimension of public relations was realised through the organisation of media-friendly 'happenings', that is, events which, in their form and content, were both attractive to journalists and (what is often the same thing) convenient for them to cover – press conferences, staged photo opportunities and walkabouts – containing little or nothing that was new in the information presented but could nonetheless be reported as 'news' by the media. The design of pseudo-events thus became an important specialist branch of the public relations profession, and 'inevitably our whole system of public information produces always more "packaged" news, more pseudo-events' (Boorstin, 1962, p. 17). Boorstin writes that:

> Pseudo-events spawn other pseudo-events in geometric progression. This is partly because every kind of pseudo-event (being planned) tends to become ritualised, with a protocol and a rigidity all its own. As each type of pseudo-event acquires this rigidity, pressures arise to produce other, derivative, forms of pseudo-event which are more fluid, more tantalising, and more interestingly ambiguous. (p. 33)

The rise of the psuedo-event is a key feature of twentieth-century politics, and of twentieth-century political journalism, and one of the reasons why public relations has been criticised by those who fear its negative impact on democracy. For critics such as Jürgen Habermas the pseudo-event, lacking in authenticity and rationality, promotes political style over substance, performance over policy, and deprives the public, consuming its pseudo-events though a compliant journalistic media, of information and meaningful choice. News becomes a form of promotion, for politics or business.

Branson's balloon

Jon Snow of *Channel 4 News* in Britain cites the example of Richard Branson's efforts to balloon himself around the world, and the ease with which this story captured the news agenda at the beginning of 1997. This, he asserts, is an example of the power of public relations to turn news into a form of advertising for big business.

Newsreader: Richard Branson's bid to be the first to go around the world by hot air balloon started in Morocco today. The tycoon said it was going to be a most magnificent adventure, but told ITN from 50 000 feet tonight that lift off had been a bit hairy. ITN's Terry Lloyd saw the launch, and he's the only journalist in the support plane following the flight.

Correspondent [over film of the lift off]: It had taken eighteen months of planning, and at last the global challenge was taking shape . . . For Branson this was to be another dream come true. The weather was good, and it was time for him to say goodbye to his wife and children . . . *[report continues in similar vein for a further three minutes]*. (*ITN News At Ten*, January 1997)

News of this sort, suggests Snow, is less about the provision of information in the public interest than the promotion of private interests:

A media mogul himself, Branson knows a picture [opportunity], a soundbite, and a concept all in the same breath. And so breathtaking is it for the news gatherer, that no pause is allowed to enable some consideration of what is actually going on. Infotainment it was. News in the old Cronkite sense of explored beginning, middle and end, it was not. (1997)

Of course, the success of such an event in gaining access to prime-time news is conditional on the readiness of journalists to accept it as a news story rather than as a piece of corporate promotion. But as the number of news outlets expands, and the amount of news time to be filled increases, it is hardly surprising that news editors are increasingly vulnerable to 'stories' which are fed to them by the public relations (PR) departments of big corporations (or small ones, for that matter). The *video news release* – prepared as a package by a private interest group specifically in order to be picked up and used in the news – is an increasingly prevalent input into news production.

British Airways and 'dirty tricks'

If Branson's balloon may be cited as an excellent example of how a news story can be 'manufactured' by a corporate actor and inserted into the mainstream news agenda with relative ease, the case of British Airways and the allegations of 'dirty tricks' made against it by a former employee presents the opposite effect – the alleged removal of 'bad news' from the journalistic agenda as the result of public relations directed, in this case, at the BBC.

The story of British Airway's (BA's) alleged 'dirty tricks' campaigns against a former employee and Virgin Airways (Richard Branson again) is a long, complex and potentially libellous one (for a detailed account, see Gregory, 1994). The important fact, for our purposes, is that a planned item on the affair by the BBC's in-depth *Newsnight* programme, having been researched and filmed for transmission in 1996, was then dropped at the last moment, reportedly after intervention by PR consultant Sir Tim Bell, and BA chairman Roger Ayling, known to be a close friend of the BBC's Director General (Gregory, 1996). Although the BBC's management denied that the dropping of the item had anything to do with the public relations efforts of Bell or Ayling on BA's behalf no other convincing explanation was offered as to why such an expensively produced segment should have suddenly been discarded on the cutting-room floor.

Reactive public relations

The above are examples of *proactive* PR, planned and coordinated with specific media objectives. But much of what public relations 'counsellors' do can be described as *reactive*, insofar as it aims to manage the news media's response to an unplanned event. Since such events are usually 'bad news' for the individual or organisation concerned, this aspect of the professional role is sometimes called *crisis management*. When a British Midland aircraft crashed at the East Midlands airport in England in December 1989 the chairman of the company appeared live on television, at the crash scene, in an effort to reassure viewers (and potential customers) that the incident was not a reflection on the airline's competence and safety. Although the cause of the accident was not then known, and neither he nor anyone else could declare with any authority what precisely had happened, the mere fact of his presence on national television was widely seen as a 'PR success' – a clear sign of the company's seriousness and calm in the face of tragedy.

Political public relations and the rise of spin

Public relations has also become central to the world of established, institutional politics and its coverage in the news. As the twentieth century progressed the various activities encapsulated within the term 'political public relations' have become ever more important in understanding how political journalism is made. Politicians have always had press officers, or 'press counsellors', and the need to present one's ideas and policies to one's 'public' is at least as old, some argue, as the reign of Charles II. In those days, the 'public' was a limited circle of upper-class, propertied men, who alone had the right to vote and exert formal influence on politics. Democracy, in the sense that I have used the term in this book, it was not.

In the twentieth century, however, as voting rights were extended and the growing power of communication media allowed the development of a transnational media environment, the concept of a 'public' deepened in the domestic arena, bringing in those (the vast majority of the population) who had hitherto been excluded from citizenship, and widened in the international arena, as political affairs and media coverage of them were 'globalised'. Considerations of 'public opinion', both at home and abroad, became much more important in policy formulation than they had ever been before and encouraged a steadily more proactive approach to political public relations and news management.

At the same time, as the expanding media's demand for stories increased, politicians found that their activities were an ideal source of material for journalists. A mutual interdependence set in, which has driven the media–politician relationship ever since.

With the help of public relations advisers, political actors began to engage in activity designed to attract the media's attention and thus generate publicity. Since the mid-1800s politicans in Europe and the United States had been giving press interviews, issuing news releases, organising photo opportunities (although these terms were not then in use) and other types of event for the benefit of the media, but these activities were peripheral to the main business of politics until the advent of mass electronic media in the post-war period made media central to the political process. From Dwight Eisenhower's 1952 presidential campaign onward each successive US president displayed a more sophisticated approach to public relations and news management than his predecessor, and the US example was followed in Britain. For the general election of 1959 the British Labour Party fought what many view as the first 'media campaign' in the United Kingdom, utilising the techniques of public relations (alongside marketing and advertising) to project their policies and image to a population quickly becoming used to the ubiquity of the media (for a history of these developments, see Cockerell, 1988; McNair, 1995).

In the United States the 1960 presidential election was the occasion of the first live television debate between the main candidates, John F. Kennedy and Richard M. Nixon. Thereafter, US politics became evermore 'media-centred', leading Boorstin, as we have seen, to coin the term 'pseudo-event' to describe happenings the main purpose of which was to attract media attention and generate positive publicity. Such events – live presidential debates; the increasingly showbiz-like party conventions; news conferences – may not have been without value as fora for the discussion of policy, but their main objective, as we saw above, was to capture and command the news agenda – they were *medialities*, pointless and irrelevant without the existence of the media to record and disseminate news of them to their audiences.

In Britain, where party conferences were once a forum for genuine and often rancorous policy debate, they have become show cases for a political brand – not advertising, because they are covered as news stories, with every detail of their organisation and presentation planned with a view to how the media, and television in particular, will report them, but 'free media', experienced by the audience not as propaganda but as news, with all the enhanced credibility which that perception brings to the moment of 'decoding'.

Public relations and journalism

Two criticisms are frequently made of the trend towards more sophisticated and intensive news management described in this chapter. First, it is argued, the picture of reality which journalism provides has been distorted by the increased use of 'medialities' or pseudo-events. The business of politics, for example, has been transformed 'from a clash of words-and-ideas conveyed in print to a contest of images-and-feelings broadcast on television' (Chagall, 1981, p. 3). In such an environment, 'appearance *is* reality' (p. 3).

Second, the journalistic reliance on sources for the provision of news, and the professional assumption that some, usually institutional, sources are automatically newsworthy, is a major cause of the news media's routine bias towards the powerful and the institutionally established. Josef Ernst observes that:

The public surveillance function of [journalism] allows for the [media] to fall prey to 'news management' by official and private interests. Because the press is compelled to report whatever is said by people holding high offices, the holders of these positions are invited to produce occasions for the purpose to be immediately reported or reproduced. (1988, p. 96)

Bias of this type is structural, arising from organisational and cultural factors which tend to privilege the powerful (see Chapter 4).

Public relations and the politics of pressure

Politics, of course, is not just about parties, and political actors are not just the party leaders and their subordinates who compete for the right to govern us. While parties are the most institutionalised, and in normal times the most powerful of political actors, we increasingly inhabit a political environment in which, through the media, all manner of non-party organisations can make meaningful and effective interventions. Fortunately, economic wealth and cultural status are not the only means of gaining access to public relations expertise and thus to the favourable media coverage which it often brings.

Pressure groups, religious and moral lobbies, businesses and trade unions, even terrorist organisations – all have shown increasing readiness to use the techniques of public relations in their attempts to shape the news, manage opinion and, ultimately, influence governmental decision-making. They are all potential *sources* in the competition to set the news agenda and define the issues around a particular debate. They are all, to this extent, proponents of *source strategies* and tactics, all players in the modern media game and significant contributors to the content of modern journalism.

As groups such as Greenpeace have shown, knowledge of how the media work and an ability to apply that knowledge to the design of media-friendly 'happenings' can be just as successful in setting the news agenda as the massed resources of a huge multinational corporation such as Shell. When the latter proposed to dump a disused oil rig stationed off the coast of Scotland in 1995 Greenpeace organised a series of non-violent, direct-action protests culminating in its members occupying the rig. Shell's efforts to evict the protesters, and the protesters' dogged resistance, provided hours of newsworthy visuals for the television journalists. As the story climbed up the news agenda in Britain and the rest of Europe, Shell found itself the target of a European-wide consumer boycott of its petroleum, and eventually had to concede defeat. Despite the expressed wishes of the British government that the Brent Spar should be buried at sea if that was what the company wanted, they were required by the power of public opinion to tow it back into land. The environmentalists had won the battle of the news agenda, and skilful news management had been their principal weapon.

Later, Greenpeace representatives admitted that the substance of their argument against Shell – that the rig would cause unacceptable damage to the sea environment in which it was to be dumped – had been untrue, or at least exaggerated, proving that the institutionally and economically powerful do not have a monopoly on the use of 'black' propaganda. By then, however, it was too late for an objective account of the Brent Spar controversy to be constructed. Public debate had moved on.

Skill in news management, then, is something that can be learnt, as well as bought, and the late twentieth century has been a period in which many organisations, lacking what Schlesinger and Tumber call the *definitional power* and *cultural capital* (Schlesinger and Tumber, 1994, p. 42) provided by wealth and institutional status, have compensated by mastering the grammar of news and exploiting the needs of the journalists. One does not, after all, require vast financial resources or political clout to understand that

- news must be produced to strict deadlines;
- journalists constantly require new material;
- journalists prefer material which can be easily packaged in the grammar and style of the particular medium being targeted;
- journalists prefer material which conforms to prevailing conventions of what news is (news values) and which, in an increasingly competitive news market, contains those elements of drama, conflict, pathos, etc. which audiences expect;
- all other things being equal, information which satisfies these demands is more likely to be reported and made into 'news' than that which is not.

To gain access to the agenda of television journalism, for example – the main prize in public relations – a story must have a strong visual component to its telling. In the case of Brent Spar, shots of speedboats being pursued across choppy northern waters, or of helicopters making hazardous landings on the deserted oil rig, were the visual elements which made the story such an attractive one for telling on television.

Tabloids, on the other hand, prefer stories with a different mix of elements: a strong human-interest angle; a whiff of personal tragedy or triumph; an opportunity for the paper's public voice to wax indignant. Armed with those understandings, and a knowledge of how to design happenings – psuedo-events – which can attract the attentions of the news media, relatively resource-poor individuals and organisations can 'break in' to the mainstream news agenda, generating coverage for a particular issue and possibly pressurising governments or other powerful institutions into making decisions which would otherwise not have been made.

As was stressed in Chapters 4 and 6, media organisations have their own institutional interests to pursue, which include being *seen* to be independent and objective and, in most cases, competitive and profitable. These imperatives create opportunities for non-elite groups – insofar as they have something 'new' to offer the journalists – to gain access to mainstream media from which they can begin to seek to influence journalistic accounts of events and issues.

Many such cases could be cited, in addition to the Greenpeace/Brent Spar example referred to above. In Britain, the antiroad lobbyists who occupied underground tunnels and held up construction work for months became a regular feature of news in 1996 and 1997. Protesters with exotic names such as 'Swampy' and 'Animal' became widely known and hugely popular, their tales of endurance in damp underground conditions coming to be seen as symbolic of youthful passion and commitment to a good cause. The events they 'manufactured' – blockades, pickets, vigils – made visually interesting television and allowed simple, dramatic stories to be told in all the media. In a political environment where environmentalism had become a respectable issue, these antiroad rebels became heroes, even in the pages of the right-of-centre tabloids.

Some 15 years earlier the women of Greenham Common also succeeded in gaining extensive media coverage for their protests against the installation of US Cruise missiles (for detailed accounts of this coverage, see GUMG, 1986). Their non-violent direct actions, such as chaining themselves to the fences of the Greenham Common air base or lying in the road to block military convoys, made exciting, dramatic television, although they never succeeded in winning the near-universal media support experienced by 'Swampy' and his colleagues, primarily because in a much more homophobic environment than now exists they were vulnerable to negative stereotyping as lesbians ('dykes') and they were operating in a much tenser political environment characterised by highly polarised ideological competition (East versus West, Warsaw Pact versus NATO, communism versus the free world, etc.) in which they were on the 'wrong' side.

Contemporary pressure groups such as the antiroad protesters often find themselves confronting established power, challenging positions which are in the materialist sense 'dominant'. This they will typically do from a 'resource-poor' position, compelling them to find ways of participating in and contributing to public debate which do not require material resources or cultural capital. For such groups, the use and manipulation of the media to communicate messages – within the framework of a news story – is potentially the most effective way of achieving this intervention. Learning to exploit the journalists' hunger for stories becomes a campaigning tool in itself, perhaps the most important campaigning tool in the postmodern, mediated political environment which characterises the times.

Even if media access is realised, however, many limitations are imposed on the protesters' message by the form of news itself. Television news, although reaching the largest number of people on a regular basis, has relatively little space for the presentation of complex ideas and arguments – simple verbal and visual images are preferred, required even, by the nature of the medium and its evolution towards ever shorter, more succinct 'bits' of information. Radio news has more time to develop stories, but no visual element to illustrate and give them resonance. Tabloid newspapers, like mainstream television news, lack the space or the inclination to cover complex subjects in depth and often assume that their readers would not be interested in or capable of absorbing such coverage. Broadsheet newspapers do contain in-depth coverage but are less likely to be seduced by the attractions of pseudo-events and 'spectaculars' and more likely to be sceptical of attempts to manipulate the news agenda.

Nevertheless, and despite these formal limitations on the presentation of the message, resource-poor organisations can achieve visibility for their causes, an important step in any campaign, given, as was noted in Chapter 3, that 'the struggle for visibility is at the centre of all politics' (Woolacott, 1996). Visibility through news coverage is not the same thing as achieving one's objectives, but it has become a precondition of campaigning success for groups without direct access to the levers of political and economic power.

Terrorism as public relations

This lesson has been learnt not only by non-violent organisations such as Greenpeace and the antiroad lobby but also by terrorist individuals and organisations. The Unabomber in America; the right-wing extremists who bombed the federal building in Oklahoma City; the IRA and other groups in Northern Ireland – all have understood that 'terrorism is an almost infallible way of achieving visibility' (Woolacott, 1996) for a cause, and have used the newsworthy properties of spectacular violence as a means of forcing their existence, and the reason for their existence, into the public domain. As a well-known media consultant puts it,

> even terrorists now have their public relations officers. At the funeral of the IRA gunman Bobby Sands, 300 camera operators and stills photographers recorded the event standing on a 25 ft high scaffolding platform specially built for them by IRA public relations personnel. (Bruce, 1992, p. 128)[4]

Baudrillard has called terrorism 'our Theatre of Cruelty' (1983, p. 114), and there is a sense in which the spectacularly violent acts of terrorist organisations can be viewed as performances for the benefit of a journalistic culture addicted to high drama. Although it does nothing to diminish the horror of bodies being blown apart by bombs in markets and office blocks, it is clear that modern terrorism is to a large extent the product of a media environment which values such acts as news items and is compelled to give those who commit them 'the oxygen of publicity', as a British government minister once described BBC coverage of the IRA. The terrorist act is the ultimate 'pseudo-event' – a politically and militarily meaningless act unless it receives recognition and coverage in the news media.

Conclusion: the source-centred approach and the sociology of journalism

As was seen in Chapter 2, a strong tradition in the sociology of journalism has emphasised the controlling, socially reproductive functions of news – its role in the ideological apparatus of capitalist societies, binding together an unequal and exploitative social system through the promulgation of a world-view which is consistent with the maintenance of dominant class interests. The sociology of sources combines with the workings of the market and the impact of new technology to undermine this instrumentalist approach to media and power.

Although, as Chapter 6 showed, there is certainly a powerful business class which controls many journalistic outlets (many more than might be thought consistent with the optimal working of democracy), the importance to the journalistic media of a steady supply of news, and news sources to supply it, and the growing technical sophistication of the news management industry, means that none of the members of that class – not Rupert Murdoch, nor Silvio Berlusconi nor Conrad Black – can dictate what the news media as a whole, nor even at times their own organs, say about events and issues. The power of news managers and other source professionals exists to a significant extent autonomously from that of owners and editors, diluting the latter's influence and creating a media environment of chaotic unpredictability rather than ordered, hierarchically structured stability.

This fact is as unsettling to establishment elites as it should be encouraging for those concerned with the health of democracy in the era of mass communication. Control of public opinion has gradually slipped away from the establishment as the breadth and range of media outlets has increased. Political power exists, of course, and at any one moment in time the composition of 'dominant groups' is easy to describe, but their stability and authority has been eroded by the mechanics and dynamics of the modern publicity process.

Of course, it is also true that the techniques of public relations and news management can help political elites to bypass democratic processes by flooding the public sphere with propaganda. There is no doubt that the activities of the public relations firm Hill and Knowlton during the Gulf War helped the Bush administration to secure a congressional majority for military intervention in Kuwait and Iraq.[5] Although the resulting conflict may have been a 'just war', insofar as any war can be just, it is clear with hindsight that 'black propaganda' and disinformation were important tools used by the politico-military establishment and by public relations companies in the context of the Gulf conflict, under contract from interested parties, to secure mass support for military actions which might otherwise have been unsympathetically received.

Public relations is also, as I have suggested, an important part of the propaganda apparatus of capitalism, selling a flawed system to domestic and global publics who now enjoy political rights which big business cannot ignore. The firm Burson Marsteller receives much of its annual turnover of more than $200 million from transnational companies anxious to maintain or improve their reputations in the face of 'bad news' stories, such as that of Union Carbide's chemical disaster in India (Beckett, 1997). One source asserts that, as of the mid-1990s, US business organisations were spending more than $1 billion per annum on environment-related public relations (Stauber and Rampton, 1995), including campaigns against pro-environmental groups and efforts to create positive, environmentally-friendly, images.

The activities – often shrouded in secrecy – of companies such as Hill and Knowlton and Burson Marsteller are often cited as evidence of the antidemocratic, propagandistic potential of public relations. As Stauber and Rampton put it,

> although the PR industry claims that it is simply participating in the democratic process and contributing to the public debate, it has to conceal most of its activities from public view if it wants to manipulate public opinion and government policy. (1995, p. 178)

Although speaking of 'it' creates a false image of the PR industry's desire or ability to function as a coherent, conspiratorial whole, and although the 'manipulation of consent' thesis downplays the vast range of socially necessary, useful activities and functions performed by public relations professionals,[6] it is obvious that, as a set of professional techniques, public relations, like medicine or jurisprudence, can be put to a variety of purposes, not all of which one might wish to support. Public relations, like journalism, has an ethical dimension, and acknowledging its emergence as a cultural factor in the twentieth century is not to give *carte blanche* to those who would abuse its power (for a discussion of ethics in public relations and journalism, see McNair, 1998). However, the growth of professional news management in the twentieth century is an index of the fact that no organisation (business, political or other), no matter how closely tied to 'the establishment', can *know* with certainty how the media are going to report its activities. If the media were part of a unitary, monolithic capitalist culture – an ideological state apparatus, as Louis Althusser once put it – public relations on behalf of government and big business would not be necessary. In authoritarian systems, where public opinion is not a meaningful category, public relations is either non-existent or lacking in credibility – perceived simply as 'propaganda' and thus lacking in persuasive power. The Chinese government used primitive and crude public relations to justify the Tienanmen Square massacre, as did Saddam Hussein to legitimise his atrocities in the Gulf. Both failed, because of the authoritarian context in which the PR was manufactured and disseminated. In advanced capitalist democracies, on the other hand, it is precisely *because* the media are open to dissenting voices, are unpredictable and contrary in their choice of and need for sources that they have become such a key arena for competitive ideological struggle and that a category of professional skilled in the techniques of that struggle has evolved to provide technical support for the participants.

This does not mean that the journalistic arena is a level playing field to which everyone has equal access. On the contrary, expertise in the techniques and skills encapsulated within the term 'public relations' has normally to be bought and paid for. Like any other commodity in the marketplace they are disproportionately available to those with the greatest financial resources, who can use them (or attempt to) to consolidate their privileged positions. There are clearly rich and poor in terms of access to public relations. Hill and Knowlton's campaign of disinformation around the Gulf War was bought for $10 million by the Kuwaiti government-in-exile. The Kurds killed a few years earlier by Hussein's gas attacks had no such resources at their disposal and found it considerably harder to have their interests represented in the news media and thence in the corridors of power. Insofar as the techniques and instruments of public relations are a resource with the potential to influence news output, they are unequally distributed throughout society in a pattern which reflects wider social inequalities of income and status. Those who are economically wealthy are also wealthy in their ability to manage the news, a fact which has alarmed some observers of journalism.

On the other hand, effective news management is not only about economic resources. As Greenpeace and others have shown, and this chapter has stressed repeatedly, skill in understanding how news works, and in designing events and happenings which can exploit that knowledge, can be just as, perhaps even more, effective in setting news agendas and securing favourable journalistic definitions of issues than can ownership and control of media. As Lasswell and Kaplan put it as long ago as 1950, 'skill, like wealth or prestige or position, is a basis of power in society and changes in the skills used in political action will have discoverable consequences for the distribution of power and influence' (1950, p. 158). The recent history of pressure-group politics throughout the advanced capitalist world supports that assertion.

9

From control to chaos: towards a new sociology of journalism

This book was conceived and written principally as a teaching and learning resource, although one which would avoid the impersonal, catch-all, cataloguing style of some textbooks. Alongside the systematic elaboration of the *factors of journalistic production,* as I have called them in this book, therefore, was an argument, or theme – that of the unpredictability and variety of journalistic responses to the events which constitute the news agenda. Chapter 2 summarised the debate within the sociology of journalism in terms of the competition–dominance dichotomy – a simplification, certainly, but one which expresses the tension between those who see journalism as, on the one hand, a facilitator of pluralistic debate, and on the other, those who see it as an instrument of conservative social control. I proposed in that chapter an alternative *'chaotic flow'* model of journalistic production, which preserved recognition of the existence of social inequality as a key feature of contemporary capitalism while incorporating the possibility, the self-evident fact, of constant challenge to, even subversion of, established power through the routine work of journalists in mainstream capitalist media. This approach was then applied in discussions of, respectively, professional ethics and culture; political pressures; the workings of the media market; the impact of new technologies; and the activities of sources and source professionals. Under these headings we saw the tendency to 'chaos rather than control' assert itself. We saw that forces beyond the influence of any individual journalist, proprietor or political–social actor drove a coverage which often challenged and undermined authority, and made effective rule by the 'rulers' who populate the dominance paradigm more difficult.

The factors of production examined above are not mutually exclusive, of course. Journalists are subject to pressures from proprietors, the competitive demands of the market, the simultaneously liberating and constraining possibilities of new communication technologies or the activities of source professionals, all at the same time. Often, the pressure from one direction may contradict that from another. The organisational constraints of journalism and the influence of professional practices such as objectivity create, as we have seen, opportunities for news management by political and social actors. The ideological preferences of a newspaper proprietor may be undermined by the competitive requirement to keep in step with readers' changing political allegiances or with public opinion. The relationship between the various factors of production may be mutually reinforcing or they may cancel each other out.

Sometimes, therefore, the journalistic production process tends to favour the powerful in society, supporting the presumptions of the dominance model. At other times, subordinate groups and views are accessed, and elites are exposed and overthrown or forced to bow to the popular will (or what some may claim the popular will to be), as in Shell's retreat over Brent Spar (see Chapter 8). Much depends on social actors' knowledge and understanding of how journalism works and their capacity to apply this knowledge to the influencing of specific journalistic media.

The impact of the factors or elements of production discussed in previous chapters may thus be to produce contradictory tendencies towards bias or neutrality in news; towards support for the establishment, or opposition to it; towards openness to non-dominant views or closure around currently dominant values. Understanding why one tendency or another will dominate in any particular story is a matter of case-by-case empirical analysis of how different factors come into play. It also requires analysis and understanding of the wider socio-economic context – the balance of political and economic forces in the domestic and international arenas. When Reagan ran the United States, for example, and the cold war was at its height, news about the Soviet Union was heavily skewed, at times even propagandistic. Now, in the absence of strategic East–West conflict, the pressures to produce 'images of the enemy' (McNair, 1988) are absent too. When wars and conflicts with clearly defined enemies *do* break out, most of our journalists return to propaganda mode, as in British and US coverage of the 1990–91 Gulf War and also in the 1998 conflict with Saddam Hussein over United Nations weapons inspections.

In general, however, advanced liberal capitalism of the North American/West European/Australasian type – economically successful, politically stable, and with an affluent, conservatively-minded proletariat not predisposed to revolution or anything like it – can afford the luxury of a dissenting journalism. Other systems, where social tensions are more acute and political power has to be exercised in an authoritarian fashion, cannot. Even in liberal democratic regimes such as Britain, as we have seen, the limits to dissent remain, policed by proprietors, politicians, the law and the force of consensual values as mediated by the journalistic profession. As we have also seen, however, continuing advances in communication technologies driven by the innovative power of capitalism make 'bad news' increasingly difficult to suppress and even more difficult to control when it is out in the public domain. Monica Lewinsky proved that in the United States, as have the widely reported misfortunes of any number of government ministers (Labour and Conservative) in Britain. The tendency of the powerful and the privileged to protect themselves by suppressing criticism is still there, and they still have substantial resources at their disposal to do so, but the competing power of the journalistic media, and those who use it skilfully, becomes ever more difficult to resist as the quantity of information in circulation, and its speed of flow, increases remorselessly. That simple fact, more than any belief in the inherent reasonableness of the system and those who run it, gives cause for realistic, empirically grounded optimism about the future of democracy and journalism's role in it.

One might go further and assert that capitalism, in the communicative advances which it has facilitated, has manufactured the means of its own chaotic democratisation, if not, as Marx predicted in the *Communist Manifesto* of 1848, sown the seeds of its own destruction. Indeed, it may be that one has prevented the other. Marx wrote that capitalism contained within it the tendency to mass pauperisation, absolute impoverishment and ultimate collapse. Eventually, he predicted, the poverty and systematic exploitation of the masses required by capitalism (and, remember, he was writing about the most advanced capitalist economies of his day) would force social revolution and progressive change towards communism. In reality, and for reasons which go beyond the scope of this book, capitalism has produced – as the precondition of its smooth reproduction – only *relative* poverty, *relative* powerlessness, *relative* exploitation, in the context of a journalistic culture which is driven, for reasons of profit, professionalism, technological possibility and public service, to expose the weaknesses of the system and its rulers in the political, economic and cultural spheres (or some of them, at least) to mass scrutiny. For this we should be grateful to our journalists, while of course reserving the right to criticise their failings. Journalists have become, notwithstanding their ideological biases, elitist world-views and restricted networks of sources, the agents of instability rather than of control.

Whether this is a good or a bad thing for the efficient governance of society is not yet clear. The chaotic flow of information about his sex life which emerged in early 1998 nearly destroyed the capacity to govern of Bill Clinton, one of the most successful (in terms of economic management) post-war US presidents. In that case the US public stepped back, raised its hands and said 'Whoa! Leave him alone. We still love him', refusing to allow the journalistic feeding frenzy to bring him down unless he was proven, beyond doubt, to be not only a 'sex addict' but a liar under oath. In other cases, such as the former Yugoslavia, there is some evidence, referred to in Chapter 7 above, that the speed of information flow – the intensity of real time news – has had negative consequences for the rational development of foreign policy by the Western powers.

As captivated audiences and concerned citizens; as political activists; as actual and potential leaders of governments, parties, public organisations and pressure groups – we are only now beginning to realise the implications for the gaining and exercise of power, for the waging of ideological struggle and the management of intellectual competition of this new journalistic environment, so different in quality from anything previously experienced. As sociologists, too, the search is on for new ways of thinking about the dynamics of the journalist–society relationship which moves beyond the dichotomies of competition–dominance, pluralist–materialist, normative–critical, to models which better express the workings of the social world in all their growing unpredictability and randomness.

This book has worked within such a model – one in which power and privilege are present, and exercise often decisive influence, but in the context of discursive struggle and contestation from a wide variety of competing perspectives. The presence and influence of 'alternative voices', I have argued, is not mere tokenism, nor a 'relative openness' which will always lead to closure in the end, but the unanticipated consequence of unrelated developments in the technologies of journalistic production and media consumption (Chapter 7); of the new 'science' of news management and its impact on journalistic practice (Chapter 8); of the evolution of increasingly media-literate audiences able to read journalistic texts critically (Chapter 3); of the fact that political independence, even subversiveness, has become a commercially sought-after 'brand' for many journalistic organisations (Chapter 6).

The model needs elaboration, but the tendency to chaos rather than control is now clear. The consequences for the future conduct of relations between journalism and society are uncertain, but watching them unfold in the coming years will be nothing if not an interesting spectator sport.

Notes

Part I. Introductions and Background

Introduction

1 The Oscar-winning account of the 1974 'Rumble in the Jungle' boxing match between Muhammad Ali and George Foreman.
2 As early as 1984 Herb Schiller was writing that

> the information sphere is becoming the pivotal point in the American economy. And, as the uses of information multiply exponentially by virtue of its greatly enhanced refinement and flexibility... information becomes a primary item for sale. (1984, p. 33)

Some 20 years on, the centrality of information and data in the global economy is self-evident.
3 For a book-length study of environmental news see Anderson (1997).
4 Thompson's brand of 'gonzo' journalism, 'a style of "reporting" based on William Faulkner's idea that the best fiction is far more true than any kind of journalism – and the best journalists have always known this' (1979, p. 114), is best encapsulated in his *Hell's Angels* (1967) and *Fear and Loathing in Las Vegas* (1972). The first published volume of Thompson's letters presents a fascinating picture of how his half-journalistic, half-novelistic style of reportage developed (*The Proud Highway*, 1997).

Kapuscinski's best work is contained in the trilogy of books about dictatorship, *The Emperor* (1984), *Shah of Shahs* (1986) and *Another Day of Life* (1987). Although these are works of reportage by a journalist in the field, much of their power resides in the aesthetic effects created by Kapuscinski's prose style.
5 Having said that, Hunter Thompson's admission in *The Proud Highway* that in his 'journalism' he had found an outlet for his novelistic ambitions seriously questions the extent to which his book-length works

(note 4) are journalism, or fiction passing itself off as journalism. Thompson's key point about gonzo journalism, on the other hand, is that it doesn't really matter.

6 For a recent account of developments in the broadcast documentary form see Kilborn and Izod (1997).

7 The 'cash-for-questions' scandal, as it became known, was covered extensively by the *Guardian* and the *Sunday Times* newspapers during the latter period of the Major Government. A detailed account of the story is given in Leigh and Vulliamy (1997).

8 The on-going debate about the tabloidisation and 'dumbing-down' of journalism which has been taking place throughout the twentieth century, and especially since Rupert Murdoch came to Britain and took over the *Sun* in the late 1960s (McNair, 1996), will be discussed at various points in this book, as we look at such issues as the impact of commercialisation and the market, or new technologies, on television news content and style. For succinct statements of the 'dumbing-down' argument see journalistic pieces by Cronkite and Snow (1997). Academic proponents of the tabloidisation thesis (and in particular of the damaging consequences of tabloidisation for the content of joualism) include Franklin (1997), Dahlgren and Sparks (1992) and, with particular reference to political journalism, Blumler and Gurevitch (1995).

9 For an introduction to the work of Laing, see *The Politics of the Family* (1971).

10 See for example work by Philip Schlesinger and Howard Tumber on the source strategies adopted by the British police (1994), and by David Miller on the source activities of the protagonists in the Northern Irish conflict (1994).

11 A discussion of the various approaches to studying journalism is given elsewhere (McNair, 1996).

12 For example, the issue of 'sleaze' which dominated the late 1990s political news agenda on both sides of the Atlantic has been condemned as a symptom of journalism's gradual loss of substance and seriousness.

The sociology of journalism

1 The introduction of the concept of the press as a fourth estate coincided with the emergence in the late eighteenth century of other key concepts in the evolution of democracy, such as 'public opinion' and the role of public debate in political decision-making. In contrast to feudal societies, where such notions were non-existent, capitalism produced 'publics' with political rights and needed a media system capable of protecting those rights, from whatever direction attacks on them might come.

2 For a more detailed account of this history see my earlier work (McNair, 1995, 1996).

3 For a detailed exposition of Habermas's theory, see his *The Structural Transformation of the Public Sphere* (1989).

4 In the traditional nuclear family a domestic environment is created within which individuals are reared in preparation for their working lives and within which they will subsist as children and adults. Not only are they fed with the energy which sustains work, they are also educated and socialised into the particular rhythms and moral disciplines of the capitalist work ethic. Until relatively recently, the family was also the site of a sex-based division of labour in which women (and their daughters, preparing for their role as adult wives and mothers) took care of unpaid domestic labour while the men went out to work in the factories and offices. Since feminist ideology began to become mainstream – a process which has still not been completed, but is clearly and unstoppably underway – the form of the 'ideal' capitalist family has begun to change, as have ideal-type sex and gender roles. One can be assured, however, that nothing will happen in the sphere of sexual politics which threatens the fundamental economic relationships of capitalist social organisation.

5 Such upheavals are the subject of Ryzsard Kapuscinski's journalism, referred to in Chapter 1, note 4.

6 The GUMG's best known work is contained in the *Bad News* (1976) and *More Bad News* (1980) volumes, sections of which are reprinted in two more recent volumes (Eldridge, 1995; Philo, 1995). For the work of the CCCS, see in particular *Policing the Crisis* (Hall et al., 1978), their study of the media's role in articulating ideas about crime, law and order and social deviance. The work of Teus Van Dijk is representative of this strand of sociology, examining among other topics the journalistic representation of emigration in Holland (1988).

7 See his essay 'Ideological state apparatuses' in Althusser (1971).

8 See in particular Chomsky and Herman (1979) and Chomsky (1988).

9 In the third volume of *Capital*, unpublished during his lifetime, Marx observed that 'the capitalists . . . confront one another only as commodity-owners' and that 'the social inter-relations of production assert themselves only as an overwhelming natural law in relation to individual free will' (1981, p. 881).

The effects of journalism

1 Quoted in *The Times*, 17 November 1993, in the context of a discussion of British newsreader Martyn Lewis's assertion that there was too much 'bad news' in the media. Rowe was further quoted as believing that there

is no such thing as good or bad news, just 'truth', which as audiences we interpret positively or negatively depending on our individual circumstances.

2 For a discussion of the encoding/decoding 'moment' in the communication process, see Stuart Hall's 1980 essay 'Encoding/decoding'.

3 See Greg Philo's *Seeing and Believing* (1990) for empirical evidence of this phenomenon.

4 Recent studies have claimed that Hollywood cinema glamorises cigarette smoking and that images of stars such as John Travolta and Samuel Jackson smoking on screen may be contributing to the growth of cigarette consumption amongst young people. If indeed this were true (and there is no 'proof'), one could argue that, unlike murder and torture, smoking is promoted and encouraged by advertisers and that the absence of any legal constraint on the activity heightens the cause–effect relationship in this case. In this respect, a link between aesthetically appealing images of smoking and smoking in real life would not be inconsistent with the 'equation' for media effects given on page 44.

5 Iyengar and Kinder note that, as with most types of effects, the impact of news on audience agendas varies according to the characteristics of the audience and the circumstances of their reception:

> When problems flare up and capture the attention of the media, agenda-setting effects show up most immediately among those directly affected by the problem. In this way, TV news reinforces and ratifies the experience of everyday life. But if coverage continues and the problem stays at the top of the media's agenda, agenda-setting effects will begin to register just as deeply among those viewers whose personal lives are untroubled by the problems given national attention (1987, p. 53).

6 Julie Flint's film, *Frontline* , was broadcast as part of the *Battered Britain* series by Channel 4 in 1995.

7 Valuable research on the genesis and media treatment of the HIV/AIDS (acquired immune deficiency syndrome) 'panic' in Britain is contained in Miller *et al.* (1998).

Part II. The Factors of Journalistic Production

The professional culture and organisational determinants of journalism

1 For historical accounts of the development of photography, and the impact of the new technology on journalism, see Goldsmith (1979) and Wells (1997).

2 Kapuscinski's best works, and those which made his reputation in the West (see note 4, Chapter 1), combine reportage with impressionistic observation and interpretation of the events being described.
3 From comments made by Mark Damazer, then Head of Weekly Programmes at the BBC's News and Current Affairs Directorate, at a conference on Media Ethics held at the University of Leeds in September 1996.

The political environment

1 Jürgen Habermas quotes Thomas McCarthy's observation that

> 'in its clash with the arcane and bureaucratic practices of the absolutist state, the emergent bourgois gradually replaced a public sphere in which the ruler's power was merely represented before the people with a sphere in which state authority was publicly monitored through informed and critical discourse by the people' (1989, p. xi).

The existence of this critical discourse, organised by the institutions of the media, acted as a guarantor of the democratic legitimacy of the post-feudal polity.
2 For example, the former head of Ostankino television, Oleg Slabynko, was shot dead in his Moscow apartment shortly after producing a documentary on governmental corruption.
3 *That Was The Week That Was* was a pioneering satirical television programme in which David Frost, amongst others, first made his name.

The economic environment

1 Another was the self-proclaimedly left-wing proprietor of regional newspapers, Owen Oyston. Convicted of rape in 1996, he, like Maxwell, embarrassed the left.
2 For an account of the *News On Sunday* fiasco, see Chippindale and Horrie (1988).
3 Famous headlines in the *Sun* and the *New York Post*, respectively, regarded as classics of the tabloid tradition (Taylor, 1991).
4 Former editor of the *Daily Mirror*, Richard Gott, argues that in the late 1980s and early 1990s 'almost all of the serious newspapers sought to meet the commercial challenge of the post-modern, post-Thatcher era by moving away from serious concerns into the essentially non-political, non-ideological world of lifestyle and "yoof"' (1996, pp. 28–33).
5 For a full account of the 'cash for questions' scandal see Leigh and Vulliamy (1997).

The technological environment

1 Harry Knowles's site, describing itself as 'the biggest, best and worst thing to happen to Hollywood since television', can be found on *www.aint-it-cool-news.com*
2 For a discussion of the impact of NICTs on censorship, see McNair, 1997.

The sociology of sources

1 Comments made in an interview for the *New Statesman* of 9 August 1996 and directed specifically at the communications managers of New Labour who, she argued, were distorting the party's message and identity.
2 This case was cited in defence of modern 'spin doctors' by Peter Mandelson in the article 'Out of the darkness', (*Guardian*, September 28, 1996).
3 Bernays's *Crystallizing Public Opinion* (1923) is one of the founding texts for the study of public relations and source strategies.
4 Brendan Bruce, the author of the book from which this quote is taken, was Director of Communications for the Conservative Party in the late 1980s.
5 The evidence for this view is overwhelming. As John MacArthur's study (1992) makes clear, officially inspired PR transformed the political environment in the United States in 1990–91.
6 For a media-studies-influenced discussion of the role of contemporary public relations see L'Etang and Pieczka (1996).

Bibliography

Adair, G. 1995: Pseudo-event's corner. *Sunday Times* 15 October.

Althusser, L. 1971: *Lenin and philosophy and other essays*. London: New Left Books.

Anderson, A. 1997: *Media, culture and the environment*. London: University College London.

Appleyard, B. 1994: Please adjust your mindset. *The Independent* 9 February.

Baistow, T. 1983: *Fourth-rate estate*. London: Comedia.

Bardoel, J. 1996: Beyond journalism: a profession between information society and civil society. *European Journal of Communication* 11 (3), 283–302.

Baudrillard, J. 1983: *In the shadow of the silent majorities . . . or to the end of the social*. New York: Semi(o)text.

Beckett, A. 1997: The acceptable face of disaster. *Guardian* 13 August.

Bernays, E. (1923): *Crystallizing public opinion*. New York: Boni and Liverigh.

Birt, J. 1996: Gateway to the BBC's future. *Guardian* 24 August.

Bloom, M. 1973: *Public relations and presidential campaigns*. New York: Thomas Crowell.

Blumler, J., Gurevitch, M. 1995: *The crisis of public communication*. London. Routledge.

Boorstin, D. 1962: *The image*. London: Weidenfeld and Nicholson.

Bourdieu, P. 1998: *On Television and Journalism*. London: Pluto.

Boyd, A. 1988: *Broadcast journalism*. London: Heinemann.

Briggs, A., Cobley, P. (eds) 1997: *The media: an introduction*. Harlow: Longman.

Bruce, B. 1992: *Images of power*. London: Kogan Page.

Bruhn-Jensen, K. 1986: *Making sense of the news*. Aarhus: Aarhus University Press.

Burn, G. 1996: *Fullalove*. London: Minerva.

Cameron, D. 1996: Style policy and style politics: a neglected aspect of the language of the news. *Media, Culture and Society* 18(2), 315–33.

Chagall, D. 1981: *The new kingmakers*. New York: Harcourt Brace Jovanovitch.

Chippindale, P., Horrie, C. 1988: *Disaster: the rise and fall of News On Sunday*. London: Sphere.

Chomsky, N. 1988: *Manufacturing consent*. New York: Pantheon.

Chomsky, N. 1989: *Necessary illusions*. London: Pluto Press.

Chomsky, N. 1992: *Necessary illusions*. London: Pluto Press.

Chomsky, N., Herman, E. 1979: *The political economy of human rights, volumes 1 and 2*. Boston: South End Press.

Cockerell, M. 1988: *Live from Number Ten*. London: Faber.

Cohen, S., Young, J. (eds) 1973: *The manufacture of news*. London: Constable.

Corner, J. 1995: *Television form and public address*. London: Arnold.

Crewe, I., Gosschalk, I. (eds) 1995: *Political communication*. Cambridge: Cambridge University Press.

Cronkite, W. 1997: More bad news. *Guardian* 27 January.

Curran, J., Seaton, J. 1997: *Power without responsibility*. 5th edition. London: Routledge.

Curran, J., Gurevitch, M. (eds) 1991: *Mass media and society*. London: Arnold.

Dahlgren, P., Sparks, C. (eds) 1992: *Journalism and popular culture*. London: Sage.

Dawkins, R. 1989: *The selfish gene*. Oxford: Oxford University Press.

Dugdale, J. 1995: Seeing and believing. *Guardian* 4 September.

Eldridge, J. (ed.) 1993: *Getting the message: news, truth and power*. London: Routledge; 1995: *Glasgow Media Group Reader*, Vol. 1. London: Routledge.

Engel, M. 1996: *Tickle the public*. London: Victor Gollancz.

Entman, R. 1989: *Democracy without citizens*. New York: Oxford University Press.

Ericson, R. V., Baranek, P. M., Chan, J. B. L. 1990: *Representing order*. Toronto: Open University Press.

Ernst, J. 1988: *The structure of political communication*. Frankfurt: European University Studies.

Fallows, J. 1996: *Breaking the news*. New York: Pantheon.

Fenton, R. W. 1966: The candidate, campaign and ballot box. *Public Relations Journal* (March).

Fiske, J. 1996: *Media matters*. London: Routledge.

Franklin, B. 1997: *Newszak and news media*. London: Arnold.

Galtung, J., Ruge, M. 1973: Structuring and selecting news. In Cohen, S., Young, J. (eds), *The manufacture of news*. London: Constable, 67–72.

Goldsmith, A. 1979: *The camera and its images*. New York: Ridge Press.

Gott, R. 1996: The newspapers we deserve. *Prospect* (July), 28–33.

Gowing, N. 1994: *Real-time television coverage of armed conflicts and diplomatic crises: does it pressure or distort foreign policy decisions?* Harvard: Harvard University Press.

Greenslade, R. 1997a: How the cult of the celebrity leads to a hierarchy of death. *Guardian* 21 July.

Greenslade, R. 1997b: The rest is waffle. *Guardian* 1 September.

Gregory, M. 1994: *Dirty tricks*. London: Little, Brown and Company.

Gregory, M. 1996: Flight from the truth. *Guardian* 30 September.

Grose, R. 1989: *The Sun-sation*. London: Angus and Robertson.

Guardian 1996: Out of the darkness. 28 September.

GUMG 1976: *Bad news*. Glasgow University Media Group. London: Routledge and Kegan Paul.

GUMG 1980: *More bad news*. Glasgow University Media Group. London: Routledge and Kegan Paul.

GUMG 1986: *War and peace news*. Glasgow University Media Group. Milton Keynes: Open University Press.

Habermas, J. 1989: *The structural transformation of the public sphere*. Cambridge: Polity Press.

Hall, S., Critcher, S., Jefferson, T., Clarke, J., Roberts, B. 1978: *Policing the crisis*. London: Macmillan.

Hall, S., Hobson, D., Lowe, A., Willis, P. (eds) 1980: *Culture, media, language*. London: Hutchinson.

Hall, S. 1980: Encoding/decoding. In Hall, S., Hobson, D., Lowe, A., Willis, P. (eds), *Culture, media, language*. London: Hutchinson, 128–38.

Hallin, D. 1986: *The uncensored war*. Oxford: Oxford University Press.

Hartley, J. 1996: *Popular reality*. London: Arnold.

Hawking, S. 1988: *A brief history of time*. New York: Bantam Books.

Iyengar, S., Kinder, D. R. 1987: *News that matters*. Chicago: University of Chicago Press.

Kapuscinski, R. 1984: *The emperor*. London: Picador.

Kapuscinski, R. 1986: *Shah of Shahs*. London: Picador.

Kapuscinski, R. 1987: *Another day of life*. London: Picador.

Katz, J. 1995: Tomorrow's world. *Guardian* 24 April.

Katz, J. 1997: Dallas gamble pays off. *Guardian* 10 March.

Kiernan, M. (ed) 1998: *Media ethics*. London: Routledge.

Kilborn, R., Izod, J. 1997: *An introduction to documentary*. Manchester: Manchester University Press.

Laing, R. D. 1971: *The politics of the family*. London: Penguin Books.

Lasswell, H., Kaplan, A. 1950: *Power and society*. New Haven: Yale University Press.

Leigh, D., Vulliamy, E. 1997: *Sleaze*. London: Fourth Estate.

L'Etang, J., Pieczka, M. (eds) 1996: *Critical perspectives in public relations*. London: International Thomson Business Press.

Lichtenberg, J. 1991: In defence of objectivity. In Curran, J., Gurevitch, (eds).

MacArthur, J. 1992: *Second front*. New York: Hill and Wang.

MacGregor, B. 1997: *Live, direct and biased?* London: Arnold.

McKie, D. 1995: 'Fact is free but comment is sacred'; or was it *The Sun* wot won it? In Crewe, I., Gosschalk, I. (eds), *Political communication*. Cambridge: Cambridge University Press, 121–36.

McNair, B. 1988: *Images of the enemy*. London: Routledge.

McNair, B. 1991: *Glasnost, perestroika and the Soviet media*. London: Routledge.

McNair, B. 1994: Media in post-Soviet Russia: an overview. *European Journal of Communication* 9 (2), 115–35.

McNair, B. 1995: *An introduction to political communication*. London: Routledge.

McNair, B. 1996: *News and journalism in the UK*. London: Routledge.

McNair, B. 1997: New technologies and the media. In Briggs, A., Cobley, P. (eds) *The media: an introduction*. Harlow: Longman, 173–91.

McNair, B. 1998: Journalism, politics and public relations: an ethical appraisal. In Kiernan, M. (ed.) *Media ethics*. London: Routledge, 49–65.

McQuail, D. 1992: *Media performance*. London: Sage.

Marx, K. 1981: *Capital,* Volume 3. London: Lawrence and Wishart.

Marx, K., Engels, F. 1976: *Collected works,* Volume 2. London: Lawrence and Wishart.

Miliband, R. 1973: *The state in capitalist society*. London: Quartet.

Miller, D. 1994: *Don't mention the war*. London: Pluto.

Miller, D., Williams, K. 1993: Negotiating HIV/AIDS information: agendas, media strategies and the news. In Eldridge, J. (ed.), *Getting the message: news, truth and power*. London: Routledge, 126–42.

Miller, D., Kitzinger, J., Williams, K., Beharrell, P. 1998: *The circuit of mass communication*. London: Sage.

Miller, J. (columnist) 1992: *Sunday Times* 9 February.

Milne, A. 1988: *DG: the memoirs of a British broadcaster*. London: Hodder and Stoughton.

Morgan, P. 1997: Piers de resistance. *Guardian* 17 February.

Murphy, D. 1991: *The stalker affair and the press*. London: Unwin Hyman.

Negrine, R. 1996: *The communication of politics*. London: Sage.

Paletz, D. 1990: *Terrorism and the media*. London: Sage.

Pearson, A. 1994: As long as it goes out live. *Independent on Sunday* 30 October.

Philo, G. 1990: *Seeing and believing*. London: Routledge.

Philo, G. 1993: From Buerk to Band Aid: the media and the 1984 Ethiopian famine. In Eldridge, J. (ed.), *Getting the message: news, truth and power*. London: Routledge, 104–25.

Philo, G., (ed) 1995: *Glasgow Media Group Reader*, Vol. 2. London: Routledge.

Pilger, J. 1997: Gutted. *Guardian* 15 February.

Ranney, A. 1983: *Channels of power*. New York: Basic Books.

Sampson, A. 1996: The crisis at the heart of our media. *British Journalism Review* 7(3), 42–51.

Schiller, D. 1981: *Objectivity and the news*. Philadelphia: University of Pennsylvania Press.

Schiller, H. 1984: *Information and the crisis economy*. Norwood: Ablex.

Schlesinger, P. 1987: *Putting reality together*. London: Routledge.

Schlesinger, P., Tumber, H. 1994: *Reporting crime*. Oxford: Clarendon Press.

Schudson, M. 1978: *Discovering news*. New York: Basic Books.

Shaw, M. 1996: *Civil society and media in global crises*. London: Pinter.

Shawcross, W. 1992: *Murdoch*. London: Simon and Schuster.

Siebert, F. 1956: *Four theories of the press*. Urbana: University of Illinois Press.

Snow, J. 1997: More bad news. *Guardian* 27 January.

Stauber, J., Rampton, S. 1995: Democracy for hire: public relations and environmental movements. *The Ecologist* 25(5), 173–80.

Taylor, S. J. 1991: *Shock! Horror! The tabloids in action*. London: Corgi.

The Times 1993: The good/bad news debate. 17 November.

Thompson, H. S. 1967: *Hell's Angels*. London: Penguin Books.

Thompson, H. S. 1972: *Fear and loathing in Las Vegas*. St Albans: Paladin.

Thompson, H. S. 1980: *The great shark hunt*. London: Picador.

Thompson, H. S. 1997: *The proud highway*. New York: Villard.

Tuchman, G. 1972: Objectivity as strategic ritual: an examination of newsmen's notions of objectivity. *American Journal of Sociology* 77(4), 660–70.

Tunstall, J. 1996: *Newspaper power*. Oxford: Clarendon Press.

Usborne, D. 1996: Murdoch meets his match. *Independent on Sunday* 24 November.

Van Dijk, T. A. 1988: *News analysis*. New Jersey: LEA.

Wells, L. (ed.) 1997: *Photography*, London: Routledge.

Welsh, T., Greenwood, W. 1997: *Essential law for journalists*. London: Butterworth.

Wolfe, T. (ed.) 1978: *The new journalism*. London: Picador.

Wolfsfeld, G. 1997: *Media and political conflict*. Cambridge: Cambridge University Press.

Woolacott, M. 1996: When invisibility means death. *Guardian* 27 April.

Yorke, I. 1995: *Television news*. London: Heinemann.

Index

ABC 20, 111
accredited witnesses 9
Ace In the Hole 11
Adair, G. 147–8
Adams, G. 40–1
advertising 35–7, 110, 148, 151–2, 170
Afghanistan 88
Africa, coverage of 79
agenda-setting 49–51
Agnew, S. 98
Aitken, J. 119
Algeria 94
Althusser, L. 27, 159, 169
Anderson, A. 167
Animal 155
Another Day of Life 167
Appleyard, B. 120
arms-to-Iraq affair 97
August 1991 coup 129, 132
Australia 104, 106, 133
Ayling, R. 150

Bad News 169
Baistow, T. 139
Bardoel, J. 134, 140
Battered Britain 170
Baudrillard, J. 157
Beckett, A. 159
Bell, Sir T. 150
Berlusconi, S. 109, 111, 142, 158
Bernays, E. 146–7, 172
Bernstein, G. 84
Bevins, A. 104
bias 31, 33, 62, 72, 45–7, 104, 106,
    109, 111, 124, 152–3, 163, 165
Bible, The 37

Big Carnival, The 11
bi-media 135
Birmingham Six 118
Birt, J. 133–5
Black, C. 142, 158
Blair, T. 40, 48, 91, 98, 100, 106,
    109–10, 115, 124
Bloom, M. 144
Blumler, J. 168
Boer war 97
Bolshevik approach to journalism 71
Boorstin, D. 147–8, 152
Bourdieu, P. 102, 112
Boyd, A. 77, 79
Branson, R. 148–50
Brent Spar 154–5, 163
Bridgewater Three 118
Brief History of Time, A 8
Britain (United Kingdom) 14, 16, 20,
    44, 47–9, 63, 70, 79, 84, 87–8,
    91–2, 95–9, 101, 105, 108–9, 111,
    113, 120–1, 123, 128, 133, 135–6,
    138, 144, 146, 151–2, 154–5, 164
British Airways 149–50
British Broadcasting Corporation (BBC)
    6, 20, 70, 92–3, 98–101, 110–11,
    120, 150, 157
British Midland 150
BBC News and Current Affairs
    Directorate 77, 122, 132–6
BBC World 133
Broadcasting Act 1990 121
Brougham, Lord H. 113
Bruce, B. 158, 178
Bruhn-Jensen, K. 13, 94
BSE, coverage of 53

Bulgaria 90
Bulger, J. 46
Burchill, J. 101
Burke, E. 20
Burn, G. 11
Burson Marsteller 159
Bush administration 97, 158

Cable Network News (CNN) 20, 102,
    111, 132–5
Cameron, D. 39
Campbell, A. 91, 98
Capital 169
Carpenter, J. 38
cash for questions 118, 168, 171
Catcher In the Rye 37
CBS 20, 111
celebrity, newsworthiness of 78
censorship 96–7, 105, 147
Centre for Contemporary Cultural
    Studies (CCCS) 26, 169
Chagall, D. 152
Challenger, coverage of 132
Channel 4 122
Channel 4 News 121, 127, 148
chaotic flow model 33, 141, 162, 165
Charles II 144, 151
Chechnya 94
China 3, 88, 129, 132, 134
Chippindale, P. 171
Chomsky, N. 27–8, 84, 87–8, 111, 169
Cityscope 137
Clifford, M. 144
Clinton, B. 18, 30, 44, 92, 165
Cockerell, M. 152
cognitive effects 34
Cohen, S. 51–2
cold war, the 87–8, 163
commentary columns 10, 47, 68
commodification 87, 112-14
Communist Manifesto, The 164
competitive paradigm 19–23, 26, 28,
    45, 103
Conservative (Tory) government 47,
    52, 96, 104, 119, 164
Conservative Party, the 44, 99–100,
    105–6, 109, 117, 121
Cook, R. 44
Coolidge, C. 146
crime, coverage of 52–3

crisis management 150
Cronkite, W. 81, 121–3, 136, 149, 168
Crystallising Public Opinion 172
Cuba 88
cultural capital 154, 156
cultural imperialism 133–4, 136
cultural relativism 72–3
Curran, J. 11, 67, 113

Dahlgen, P. 168
Daily Mail 96, 118
Daily Mirror 115–16, 171
Daily Sport 38, 116
Daily Star 116
Daily Telegraph 108
Dallas Morning News 138
Damazer, M. 171
dangerous dogs, coverage of 52, 54
Dawkins, R. 30
Day Today, The 120
definitional power 154
deviation, newsworthiness of 77–8, 81
Diana, Princess of Wales 11, 48–9,
    78–9, 95
digitalisation 100, 128, 134–6, 140
documentary 4, 7, 9
dominance paradigm 19, 21–6, 38,
    31–3, 45, 72, 163
Drudge Report, The 70, 141
Dugdale, J. 122
dumbing down 18, 56, 114, 168
Dunblane 47–8, 51

editorials 10, 38, 47, 53, 68
Einstein, A. 72
Eisenhower, D. 151
Emperor, The 167
encoding/decoding 39, 170
Engels, F. 26–7
Entman, R. 50, 66, 69, 76–7
environmental news 62–3
Ericson, R. V. 70
Ernst, J. 82, 152–3
ethics 64–5
Ethiopian famine, 1984 43, 50

Fallows, J. 56
Faulkner, W. 74
Fear and Loathing in Las Vegas 74,
    167

features 8–9
feature films 37
feminism 31, 46
Fenton, R. W. 146
fiction 7, 64, 75
First World War 145
Fiske, J. 23, 26, 38, 46–7
Flint, J. 53, 170
Flowers, G. 92
food panics 52–3
Forza Italia 109, 111
fourth estate 19, 28, 112, 118–19
Fox 20, 111
France 84, 91–2, 132–3
Frank Magid Associates 120
Franklin, B. 168
Freedom of Information Act 1998 91
French revolution 21
Frontline 170
Frost, D. 171
Fullalove 11

Gaddaffi, M. 88
Galtung, J. 77
general elections, coverage of:
    1959 151
    1987 106
    1992 106
    1997 98, 100, 102, 105–6, 110, 115
General Strike of 1926, coverage of 99
German Ideology, The 26
Glasgow University Media Group
    (GUMG) 26, 63, 155, 169
globalisation 131–4, 136
Golding, P. 16
Goldsmith, A. 170
gonzo journalism 74–5
Gorbachev, M. 129–32
Gott, R. 171
Gowing, N. 130
Gramsci, A. 27
Greenham Common 155
Greenpeace 153–5, 157, 160
Greenslade, R. 77, 79, 118
Greenwood, W. 95
Greer, I. 144
Gregory, M. 150
Grenada 97
Grose, C. 115
Guardian 11, 84, 108–9, 116, 118–19

Guildford Four 118
Gulf war 97, 132, 158, 160, 164
Gurevitch, M. 168

Habermas, J. 21, 113–14, 148, 169,
    171
La Haine 38
Haiti 86
Hale-Bopp 8
Hall, S. 26, 170
Hallin, D. 72
Halloween 37
Hamilton, N. 119
Hart, G. 92
Hartley, J. 17, 116
Hawke, B. 106
Hawking, S. 8
health scares 53–4
Heisenberg's Uncertainty Principle 72
Hell's Angels 74, 167
Herman, E. 27–8, 84, 87–8, 111, 169
Hill, A. 4
Hill and Knowlton 158–60
historical materialism 26
HIV/AIDS, coverage of 55, 86, 170
Hofstetter, R. 75
homophobia 31
Horrie, C. 171
Hussein, S. 88, 132, 160, 164
hypodermic model 35

ideological interpellation 27
ideology 5–7, 16, 22–3, 25–6, 29–31,
    40, 46, 57, 66, 71–2, 86, 88, 103
impartiality 70, 91, 94, 111, 119
Independent Television News (ITN) 80,
    93, 110–11, 120, 136
industrial news 63
infotainment 120–1, 127, 149
Internet 9–11, 88, 123, 125, 128,
    135–42
Internews 90
interpretive frameworks 25, 40–3, 88
interviews 10
Iran 88
Irangate 97, 118
Irish Republican Army (IRA) 70, 96,
    157
Italy 95, 111
ITV 122

Iyengar, S. 50, 170
Izod, J. 168

John, E. 78

Kaplan, A. 160–1
Kapuscinski, R. 7, 75, 167, 169, 171
Kassovitz, M. 38
Katz, J. 137, 139–40, 142
Keeler, C. 115
Kennedy, J. F. 30, 152
Kholodov, D. 94
Kilborn, R. 168
Kinder, D. R. 50, 170
Knowles, H. 141, 172
Korea 88

Labour government 91, 96, 100, 106,
    141, 164
Labour Party 47, 98–100, 102, 104–6,
    108–10, 115, 144, 151
labour movement, coverage of 105
Laing, R. D. 12, 168
Lasswell, H. 160–1
Lawrence, S. 118
Leigh, D. 168, 171
Lenin, V. I. 29, 71, 82, 86
L'Etang, J. 172
Leveller, The 113
Lewinsky, M. 18, 44, 47, 70, 92, 118,
    141, 164
Lewis, M. 79, 169
Libya 50
Lichtenberg, J. 68, 75–6
Live Aid 44
lobby, the 91
lobbying 15, 63, 97–100, 119
Lockerbie bombing 49–50
Los Angeles Police Department 46
Los Angeles riots, 1994 44

MacArthur, J. 172
McCarthy, T. 171
MacGregor, B. 127
Mackenzie, K. 104, 107
McKie, D. 104
McNair, B. 56, 71, 86–7, 89, 91, 112,
    152, 159, 163, 168–8, 172
McQuail, D. 83
McVeigh, T. 137

Major government 100
Major, J. 97, 106
Mandelson, P. 144, 172
Marshall Plan of the Mind 80
Martin, B. 78
Marx, K. 26–30, 32, 164, 169
marxism 71–2
materialism 26–7, 71–3
Maxwell, R. 95–6, 104, 171
medialities 152
memes 30, 33
Merchant, P. 44
Microsoft 5, 137
Middle East, coverage of 89
Middle East, journalism in 94
Miliband, R. 84, 123
Miller, D. 143, 168, 170
Miller, J. 105, 108
Milne, A. 99
miners' strike, 1984–5 42–63
Mitterand, F. 92
moral panic 51–55
More Bad News 169
Morgan, P. 116
Morris, D. 144
Moscow Radio 132
Moskovsky Komsomolets 94
Murdoch, E. 103
Murdoch, R. 30, 98, 100, 102–6, 108,
    110, 114, 124, 133, 142, 158, 168
Murdock, G. 16
Murphy, D. 76

Nation, The 56
National Enquirer 38, 117
National Security State 27–111
Natural Born Killers 38
NBC 20, 111
Negrine, R. 63
Neil, A. 104, 108
new journalism 4, 39, 73–5
New Labour 24, 106, 110, 124, 172
New Statesman 168, 172
New York Post 171
News At Ten 80, 148
News Corporation 110, 135
news grammar 80–1
News International 78, 100, 104, 106,
    109–10

news management 6, 15, 50, 55, 98, 144, 151–4, 158–60, 163, 166
Newsnight 150
News of the World 106
News on Sunday 108, 171
news values 12, 13, 25, 77–81, 86, 95, 121–2, 133, 154
Newsweek 70
Nixon, R. M. 74, 98, 152
normative approach 19, 45, 69
Northern Irish conflict, coverage of 40–2, 96
Northern Ireland peace agreement, 1988 96

objectivity 5, 12–13, 64–77, 87, 89, 111, 119, 132, 134, 163
Oklahoma bombing 134, 137, 157
on-line newspapers 137–8, 140–1
organisational effects 55–7
ownership 14–15, 20, 24, 28, 92–8, 98, 101–12, 119, 123, 135, 160
Oyston, O. 171

Panorama 97, 98
Pearson, A. 120
Pepys, S. 144
Philo, G. 170
photography 67, 126
Pieczka, M. 172
Pilger, J. 116
pluralism 19–22, 26, 29, 65, 69, 84, 86, 89, 108, 123
Pol Pot 70
Policing the Crisis 169
political culture 89–94
political system, 88–9, 94
politico-economic approach 16
Politics of the Family, The 168
Poor Man's Guardian, The 113
positivism 66
postmodernism 4, 32, 156
Pravda 104
preferred reading 45
presssure groups 153, 156
Prince Charles 122
Private Eye 104
Profumo scandal 115
propaganda model 27
Proud Highway, The 167

proximity, newsworthiness of 77–8
pseudo-events 147–8, 152, 155–7
public relations 6, 17, 97–8, 130, 143–8
public sphere(s) 21, 55, 112, 114, 116, 122, 127, 142, 145, 158
pundits 10, 71

Queen, the 148

racism 7, 31, 46
Radio 4 122
Radio 5 Live 122, 135
Radio Liberty/Radio Free Europe 92, 131
Rampton, S. 159
Ranney, A. 75
rapid rebuttal 98
Reagan Administration 97
Reagan, R. 104, 163
Real Lives 97
real-time news 126–8, 130–2, 165
Representation of the People Act 95
Reservoir Dogs 44
Romania 90
Rousseau, J. J. 144
Rowe, D. 35, 42, 169–70
royal family 48, 95, 116, 122, 124
Ruge, M. 77
Russia 13–14, 88–91, 93–4

Safire, W. 101
Salinger, J. D. 37
Sampson, A. 114, 142
Saudi Arabia, 3, 134
Schiller, D. 67, 113
Schiller, H. 167
schizophrenia 12
Schlesinger, P. 62, 154
Schudson, M. 113
Scorsese, M. 37
Sexton, J. 67, 113
Second World War 20, 70, 87, 103, 126, 131
Seeing and Believing 170
Selfish Gene, The 30
sexism 7, 46
Shah of Shahs 167
Shawcross, W. 103
Shell 153–4, 163

Short, C. 144
Siebert, F. 69
Simpson, O. J. 46, 100
Sinn Fein 40–1, 96
Sky News 110, 122, 136
Slabynko, O. 171
Slate 138
sleaze, coverage of 96, 106, 168
Snow, J. 121–2, 127–8, 146–9, 168
Somalia 130
sources 6–8, 75–7, 143–61
South Africa 28–9, 86, 94
Soviet bloc countries 88, 105
Soviet Union, approach to journalism
    of 71, 86, 89, 104, 129, 131
Soviet Union, coverage of 87, 163
Sparks, C. 168
Spectator, The 108
spin doctors 15, 143
spin doctoring 98
Springer, A. 142
Stalin, J. V. 86
Stauber, J. 159
Stone, O. 38
Straw, W. 141
*Structural Transformation of the Public
    Sphere, The* 169
Suez crisis, coverage of 99
Sun, The 11, 47, 104, 106, 108, 110,
    115–16, 168, 171
Sunday Times, The 105, 108, 110, 118
Sutcliffe, P. 96
Swampy 155

tabloidisation 116, 119–23, 166
tabloids 38, 47–8, 68, 96, 108, 115–18,
    121–2, 135–6
Taiwan 88
Tarantino, Q. 37, 44
Taylor, S. 118, 171
telegraph 126, 137
terrorism 157
That Was The Week That Was 98, 171
Thatcher, M. 97–8, 104, 106, 115
Thompson, H. 4, 7, 10, 74–5, 101, 167
Tienanmen Square 129, 160
Time-Warner 111
Times, The 108

trade unions 153
Tuchman, G. 68
Tumber, H. 154, 168
Turner, T. 102, 111, 132–3

Unabomber 157
Union Carbide 159
United States of (America) 3–4, 14, 16,
    20, 39, 43–4, 46, 66, 70, 78, 84,
    87, 89–92, 95, 97, 100–2, 104,
    108, 110–11, 113, 117, 118–20,
    122, 128, 131–3, 138, 141, 144,
    146, 151–2, 163–4
United States Information Agency
    (USIA) 92
Usborne, D. 102

Van Dijk, T. 169
Versace, G. 78
video news release 149
Voice of America 131
Vulliamy, E. 168, 171

Watergate 11, 84, 97–8, 118–19
Wells, C. 170
Welsh, T. 95
Westland affair 97
When We Were Kings 4
Whitlam, G. 104
Wilder, B. 11
Williams, K. 143
Wirthlin, R. 144
Wolfe, T. 4, 74
Wolfsfeld, G. 89–90
Woodward, C. 84
Woolacott, M. 49, 156–7
Workingman's Friend, The 113
World Service 132–3

Yeltsin, B. 90
Yesterday's Men 99
Yorke, I. 127
Young, H. 101
Young, J. 51
Yugoslavia 88, 130, 165

Zhirinovsky, V. 90
Zhuganov, G. 90